Living
Church

Living Church Series
J. Dwight Stinnett, series editor

Available now . . .

Vital Spirit, Vital Service
Spirituality That Works
Trinette V. McCray

Learning Mission, Living Mission
Churches That Work
Glynis LaBarre

Empowering Laity, Engaging Leaders
Tapping the Root for Ministry
Susan Gillies and M. Ingrid Dvirnak

Caring Pastors, Caring People
Equipping Your Church for Pastoral Care
Marvin A. McMickle

Making Friends, Making Disciples
Growing Your Church through Authentic Relationships
Lee B. Spitzer

www.judsonpress.com / 800-4-JUDSON

Vital Spirit, Vital Service

Spirituality That Works

TRINETTE V. McCRAY

J. DWIGHT STINNETT, SERIES EDITOR
FOREWORD BY KIRK BYRON JONES

Living
Church

JUDSON PRESS
PUBLISHERS SINCE 1824

Join our mailing list for updates and special offers.
www.judsonpress.com/mailing_list.cfm

BU
4501.3
.M33185
2014

Vital Spirit, Vital Service: Spirituality That Works
© 2014 by Judson Press, Valley Forge, PA 19482-0851
All rights reserved.

Interior design by Wendy Ronga, Hampton Design Group.
Cover design by Tobias Becker and Birdbox Graphic Design.

Library of Congress Cataloging-in-Publication data
McCray, Trinette V.
Vital spirit, vital service: spirituality that works / Trinette V. McCray. – first [edition]. pages cm.–(Living church) Includes bibliographical references. ISBN 978-0-8170-1754-5 (pbk.: alk. paper) 1. Spirituality–Christianity. 2. Spiritual life–Christianity. 3. Christian life. 4. Christianity and culture. 5. Pastoral theology. 6. Christian leadership. I. Title.
BV4501.3.M33185 2014
248.4–dc23   2014008422

Printed in the U.S.A.
First printing, 2014.

Contents

Foreword   vii

Preface to the Series   ix

Introduction   xii

1. Christian Spirituality Basics   1

2. What Is This Spirituality?   22

3. Spirituality Present in Scripture   29

4. Spirituality across Time and Cultures   50

5. From Prayer Closet to Food Pantry, from Asceticism to Activism   74

6. Spirituality That Works: Contextual, Cultural, and in Community   80

7. Spirituality That Works: Relevant, Relational, and Rejuvenating   91

8. Learning from One Another   98

9. Putting the Principles into Action   123

10. Active Spirituality and Christian Discipleship   144

Appendix: Assessment Guide   152

It is my honor to dedicate this book

to all the spiritual and life giants

whom God sent to me to help form and shape

my life—the greatest among them being

James and Ruth McCray, my mom and dad,

and Irene B. Gardner, my Big Mama.

Foreword

Living Church

Having been inspired to become a minister as a youth, in part, by the enchanting social clerical witness of Martin Luther King Jr., and having recovered from a bout with professional burnout through the soulful literary mentorship of Howard Thurman, I am especially interested in a book that seeks to blend deliberate activism with deepening spirituality. In *Vital Spirit, Vital Service*, Trinette V. McCray identifies such a blending as "spiritual activism." Because such is a model worth reexamining and re-creating in today's world, *Vital Spirit, Vital Service* is a book worth reading.

First, *Vital Spirit, Vital Service* succinctly summarizes some of the very best examples of spiritual activism, from the Old Testament prophets to Jesus, to more recent examples, such as Martin Luther King Jr., Dietrich Bonhoeffer, Fannie Lou Hamer, Dorothy Day, and Jitsuo Morikawa. Common and and commendable to each is the avoidance of overly individualistic and overly ecclesiastical faith expression. The church is to matter as much to society as it does to persons, and to other institutions as much as it does to itself. Because sometimes we have to step back before we can move forward, revisiting well-known and not-so-well-known models of spiritual activism is a significant endeavor.

Second, *Vital Spirit, Vital Service* is more than a survey of applaudable social ministry models. McCray makes her work instantly vital to churches by providing readily understood categories and guides for understanding, communicating, and evaluating a church's current spiritual activism. Perhaps the most important of these tools are her Spheres of Significance:

Personal Significance with God
Significance with Self and Others
Significance with Faith Community
Significance with Community and Institutions
Significance with Creation and Global Community

While reading this thoughtful and practical section, I immediately began to think of ways I might use this helpful framework with the amazing church fellowship I have recently been called to serve as interim pastor.

Supreme sage and activist Abraham Joshua Heschel is said to have reflected on his march from Selma to Montgomery: "I felt my legs were praying." *Vital Spirit, Vital Service* will help more of us to experience what Heschel did, more often. To engage social action in a spirit of fervent prayerfulness is to enhance the effectiveness of such action and bring us closer to a realization of what Martin Luther King Jr. called the "beloved community." Moreover, when what one does as an act of deliberate social justice—making feels like prayer, the prized life gem of personal *meaning* and *fulfillment* is well within reach, as well.

—Kirk Byron Jones, DMin, PhD
Author of *Rest in the Storm:
Self-care Strategies for Clergy & Other Caregivers* and
*Refill: Meditations for Leading with Wisdom,
Peace, and Joy* among other titles!

Preface to the Series

"What happened? Just a few years ago we were a strong church. Now we're not sure if we can survive another year."

It is a painful conversation I have had with more church leaders than I can name here.

Images such as *meltdown, tsunami, earthquake,* and *storm* have been used to describe the crisis developing in the North American church over the last 25 years. Our present crisis is underscored by the American Religious Identification Survey 2008. Not just one local congregation, but nearly every church is being swamped by the changes.

Volumes have already been written in analysis of the current situation and in critique of the church. I suggested a few books and workshops that I knew, but the church leader with whom I was talking was overwhelmed by all the analysis. "Yes, I am sure that is true. But what do we do? When I look at what is happening and I hear all the criticism, I wonder if the church has a future at all. Do we deserve one?"

I emphasized that there are no simple answers and that those who offer simplistic solutions are either deceived or deceiving. There is no "church cookbook" for today (and I'm not sure there ever really was one). I tried to avoid an equally simplistic pietistic answer.

Still, the church leader pressed. "So is the church dead? Do we just need to schedule a funeral and get over it?"

I do not accept the sentiment of futility and despair about the future of the church. I believe the church persists not because of what we do, but because of what God has done and continues to do in the church.

The pain is real, however, as are the struggle and the longing. I wanted to help church leaders such as this one understand, but not be overwhelmed by the peculiar set of forces impacting the church today. But information was not enough. I wanted to encourage them with specific things that can be done, without implying that success is guaranteed or that human effort is sufficient. I wanted them to learn from what others are doing, not to copy them mechanically, but to use what others are doing as eyeglasses to look closely at their own context. I wanted them to avoid all the churchy labels that are out there, and be a living church in their community, empowered and sustained by the living God.

Those of us who work with groups of churches and who pay attention to the things that are happening around us know that several forces are having a devastating affect on the church today. Both formal studies and personal observation identify at least eight key areas where the impact has been especially acute.

These areas are biblical illiteracy, financial pressures, overwhelming diversity, shrinking numbers, declining leadership base, brokenness in and around us, narrowing inward focus, and unraveling of spiritual community. It is not hard to see how each of these is related to the others.

Living Church is a series from Judson Press intended to address each of these forces from a congregational perspective. While our authors are well-informed biblically, theologically, and topically, these volumes are not intended to be an exercise in ecclesiastical academics. Our intent is to empower congregational leaders (both clergy and laity) to rise to the challenge before us.

Our goal is not merely to lament our state of crisis, but to identify creative and constructive strategies for our time and place so that we can move on to effective responses. Our time and place is the American church in the twenty-first century.

The first volume in this series, *Making Friends, Making Disciples*, by Dr. Lee Spitzer, addresses the issue of shrinking numbers by reminding us of the spiritual discipline of being and making friends, not with some ulterior motive, but because God has called us to relationship.

The second volume, *Caring Pastors, Caring People*, by Dr. Marvin

McMickle, confronts the growing brokenness within and around the church by challenging leaders who will reach out to provide pastoral care, both within the congregation and then in the community beyond.

The third volume, *Empowering Laity, Engaging Leaders*, by Susan Gillies and Ingrid Dvirnak, considers the declining leadership base in many churches today and asserts, "Church vitality depends on the involvement of both clergy and laity in meaningful ministry."

The fourth volume, *Learning Mission, Living Mission*, by Glynis LaBarre, argues that, at its core, mission is about demonstrating the Reign of God. The church must travel with and learn from its surrounding community to become the missional church God has called us to be.

This fifth volume, *Vital Spirit, Vital Service: Spirituality That Works*, by Dr. Trinette McCray, dives into the deep waters of Christian spirituality with her call to live "undivided and integrated lives where all we do is an expression of our faith." This important task challenges our media-saturated world, confronts counterfeit "spiritualities," and connects the church to its unique source of power. This book is especially relevant in an era that revels in "spirituality" but eschews "religion."

Vital Spirit, Vital Service is a different kind of book on spirituality. It is neither an encyclopedia of practices nor a guidebook to arcane individualistic exercises. While presenting a spirituality of activism, Trinette notes that "significance does not begin with our doing . . . but knowing that we have been embraced by God's love." She is unambiguously Christian. She is clearly biblical. Her activist approach to spirituality moves seamlessly from our personal relationship with God to our concern for all creation and the global community. She pauses by and learns from the likes of Dietrich Bonhoeffer, Dorothy Day, Fannie Lou Hamer, Martin Luther King Jr., and Jitsuo Morikawa. Underlying all is her conviction that "the church is called to be the presence of Christ among people in community and in relationship with others." Amen.

—Rev. Dr. J. Dwight Stinnett, Series Editor
Executive Minister, American Baptist Churches,
Great Rivers Region

Introduction

> People are the basis of our significance. Our significance
> does not depend upon the grateful appreciation of indi-
> viduals. But rather, it comes from the fact that we have
> touched one of God's creations in a personal way.
>
> —Eldon Fry[1]

During the course of my ministry, I have shared with a variety of groups of people: youth and young adults, college students, women of all ages and stages in life, men in mid to late career, the newly retired, and seniors. In each of these groups a common question surfaces as our conversation deepens. Students and teens frequently visit questions around their purpose and place in the world and how the answers impact the choices they must make. Women and men who are midway through their life journeys evaluate whether they are spending their time doing what truly matters to them the most. I met with an elderly woman and had the chance to hear her questions around how she can serve in her church in a way that makes meaning for her at this stage in her life. Theirs are common inquiries indeed. Teens are impacted by many voices seeking to influence their choices and direction. Adults are immersed in day-to-day chatter and cares.

On one occasion when I was leading a discussion among college students on trends in our culture, the conversation turned toward the intense level of information, media, and external stimulation we all experience. The students talked about the mediums they are immersed in, such as viewing tweets and Facebook posts and surfing the Internet and the many cable news media outlets. I had to acknowledge that I, too, become overly engaged with the many available media connections. Researchers, social scientists, and cultural examiners have labeled this existence a "media-saturated culture." While technology offers us many ways to communicate and "connect" virtually, true and authentic relationship happens in the strongest way through presence and personal contact. It is our ability to be seen, known, and touched that makes way for wholeness.

Media saturation is a challenge that is facing the church today. Within the context of our own spirituality, the obvious question is, how so? How is the church's message challenged? How are persons who are seeking to lead strong lives as Christ's disciples impacted? In what ways is the world we seek to reach impacted by such saturation?

Mouthpi3ce, a Christian rap group of millennials and "cultural thinkers," speaking through a song released in 2012 titled "Turn It Off,"[2] is an inspiring voice from this generation pointing out the cultural lures they face and the gospel life they are challenged to live.

I became aware of this song when it was a part of a skit performed by the youth at Calvary Baptist Church in Milwaukee during their 2013 Youth Sunday worship. Their dramatic praise and dance portrayal of the point of "Turn It Off" delivered a powerful message not only for youth but for adults as well. I was struck by the lyrics that point to some of the messages coming through many media on television, for example that are inconsistent with spiritual living. The Calvary youth urged the congregation, regardless of age, to attend to their spiritual life by exercising judgment and discernment as to what is good and what is compromising. They stressed that the Holy Spirit aids us in sorting through what we hear and what we do.

Spirituality and Significance amid the Chatter

Emerging through these mediums are a diverse variety of opinions, positions, theories, thought patterns, and persuasions. Certainly media and social networking are increasingly valuable tools for the church and are useful for Christian witness and spiritual growth. Is the church, though, just one voice among many? Whether by our own doing or by media's mere presence, it is difficult to escape media's grasp and, at times, captivation. Although media can be useful, a personal result of being immersed in a media-saturated culture is the potential loss of our own *sense of significance* at many levels.

While being so connected, many I talk to wonder, *How do I matter? Where do I fit in?* and *What really counts for me?* All are good and worthy questions to explore, for significance—having meaning, purpose, and consequence—is very important. Living lives of consequence, a pursuit to live from the inside out, is as relevant for people living in the twenty-first century as it was for those in centuries past. Who we are—our *being*, our spirit and soul—is central to our significance.

It is vital, then, to understand that for the Christian true significance is a matter of spirituality. It's about how we relate to God, ourselves, our neighbors, and all of creation. Our times breed a yearning for authentic significance that is real, felt, and transformative from the inside out. At the heart of this book's message is the answer that spirituality brings to a yearning experienced by many in our churches just as much as it is in the wider culture today—a yearning to feel and be and live with significance. A connection exists between our own spirituality and our sense of person and place that makes living a significant life good discipleship. Our spirituality, when actively engaged, can lead us to that place of having, as Eldon Fry says, "touched one of God's creations in a personal way" heart to heart, spirit to spirit, soul to soul. This personal way is not fully accomplished through media connections.

Our spirituality is something that goes along with us wherever we go—into our churches, homes, communities, clubs, schools, and workplaces. It is best practiced and lived in community, not in isolation. The church needs to recognize and cultivate this perspective, for the church is called to equip and empower people to make the connections between their Christian spirituality and their soul's capacity to "touch one of God's creations in a personal way."

How do we do so? One prime way this hands-on spirituality happens is through the service we give. How we serve is an expression of who we are. An old traditional song sung most in the African American experience rings true here, "If I Can Help Somebody," most strongly expresses how the service we give to others gives our lives significance.[3] This song is a favorite for tribute services and recognition programs because it articulates very well the connection between significance and serving as a practiced hands-on spirituality.

Strengthening the connection between spirituality and serving is critical for making disciples in the church today. Disciple making is teaching laypeople to carry kingdom principles such as love of neighbor, justice, peace, mercy, and hope into the world—a world of institutions, workplaces, communities, schools, and families.

Fundamentally, the question is how can our spirituality give our lives significance in this climate of chatter, noise, and diverse messages that sometimes conflict with our calling to serve as the hands and feet of Christ in a personal way and not in isolation?

Tobias Bass from Oklahoma gives us a prime example of how spirituality can give our lives significance in today's world. As a ten-year-old, Tobias understood what it means to live helping others. His older brother, Titus, has cerebral palsy and is unable to walk, which would bring Titus to tears when he saw other children playing outside. Tobias wrote to a local television station to ask them to help him find someone who could loan him a jogger's stroller, and he received one as a gift from a viewer after an outpouring of stroller offers. Tobias is committed not only to being God's hands and feet, as his pastor encourages people to be, but "I'm going be his legs too," he says, by serving as his brother's feet and legs. Further, Tobias invites parents to ask him to take their disabled children for runs in the stroller. In his letter he writes, "I can be the legs for more than one kid," he says. His motivation to live with such great impact comes from his spirituality. "I am going to be a pastor someday and my mentor is Pastor Craig Brochel of Life Church. So I'm spiritually prepared."[4]

A New Paradigm for Christian Personal Identity

Through this volume, I will introduce a new paradigm for Christian identity that underpins and influences our framework for living. In this paradigm, I underscore three understandings about our Christian identity.

Discipleship Is More Than Salvation

The Christian life begins with our belief in Jesus Christ as the Son of God and acceptance of his blood for the forgiveness of our sin as Lord and Savior. Our submission to Jesus' lordship is our response to his call to follow him with our lives, our gifts, our wills, and our talents in service to him to fulfill God's purposes in the world. It is in our discipleship that we commit our hands and our feet to touch God's creation in a personal way. And we are enabled to serve as the community of faith provides opportunities for deepening, equipping, and ministering in the practices it adopts. These are the three practices Jeffery D. Jones identifies as keys to disciple forming in his essay "Practices in the Disciple-Forming Community." He does not see them operating separately, but integrally as a holistic practice of formation.[5] The local church is a disciple-forming community that exists to obey Jesus' great commission to "make disciples of all nations, baptizing them in the name of the Father and of the Son and of the Holy Spirit, and teaching them to obey everything I have commanded you" (Matthew 28:19-20). We are to go beyond salvation, which is a free gift and the redemptive aim of God, to our next goal of true discipleship.

Spirituality Is More Than Sanctification

Sanctification—that is, to be set apart for a special use, for a special purpose, for a holy life—is to walk in our certain callings from God that give life expression and meaning. Spirituality engages us, enlivens us, and enlists us in the path of God's purpose for us in the world—that is, our callings—and thereby our significance. We are set apart to serve as the hands and feet of Christ, touching God's creation in a personal way.

Our Christian faith offers us a discipline that guides us along the path toward achieving spiritual and personal significance through living a spirituality that leads us to be present and engaged in our surroundings. In such a place, we can touch and be touched, feel and be felt, heal and be healed, and ultimately love and be loved. Our own spiritual practices and disciplines ought to bring to us these things as a grace, giving us a passion that goes beyond simple disciplines. We need to seek individual disciplines and practices that connect in practical and relevant ways to stir up, support, and sustain an active and engaged faith.

Transformation Begins with Activism Here and Now
Rather than waiting for glorification later, Christians are called to be present in the world in a transformative way in the here and now. Do not wait for things to become better with a "pie in the sky by and by" sense of waiting for all things to be made right in the restored world. We are to pray, "Thy kingdom come; thy will be done on earth as it is in heaven," and act with our hands and our feet joined with God's power to fulfill God's purpose on earth. We are to follow up in the twenty-first century the legacy of the Great Awakening, the social gospel movement, and the civil rights movement of former times. Our actions must flow from the theology, inspiration, and activism of Walter Rauschenbusch, Helen Barrett Montgomery, Martin Luther King Jr., Fannie Lou Hammer, Joan Chittister, and Jim Wallis.

Today we hear the voices of Shane Claiborne in his book *The Irresistible Revolution: Living as an Ordinary Radical*,[6] Adam Taylor in his book *Mobilizing Hope: Faith-Inspired Activism for a Post-Civil Rights Generation*,[7] and Deena Guzder in her book *Divine Rebels: American Christian Activists for Social Justice*.[8] The messages and positions espoused by these leaders continue to encourage the significance of personal spirituality in motivating and sustaining social transformation.

I am inspired by the model of Martin Luther King Jr., who aligned greatness with serving in his sermon "The Drum Major Instinct."[9] An active spirituality that serves is the key to this kind of spiritual and personal significance. Jesus put emphasis on greatness in this way: "Whoever wishes to be great among you must be your servant" (Matthew 20:26 NRSV).

The chapters in this book will examine and discuss the aspects of the development of this spirituality beginning with a brief overview of Christian spirituality basics (chapter 1) and definitions and description of hands-on spirituality (chapter 2). We will see how spirituality evolves through Scripture (chapter 3) and examine spirituality across time and cultures (chapter 4). This hands-on spirituality that gives life significance will take us from the prayer closet to the food pantry as we move from asceticism to activism (chapter 5).

We will then more deeply discuss this spirituality that works contextually, culturally, and in community (chapter 6). And we will see that spirituality that works is at its core relevant, relational, and rejuvenating of persons, church, community, and other contexts (chapter 7). Looking at best ministry practices from local church and denominational examples in chapter 8, we will see that the church becomes a community of practice with opportunities to learn from one another. We will note principles that emerge as centerpieces for discipleship ministry and see how to put them in action to form lives of personal and spiritual significance (chapter 9). Finally, we will acknowledge that the resulting active spirituality fundamental to Christian discipleship must be nurtured and sustained through practices of renewal, Sabbath, and retreat (chapter 10).

Notes

1. Eldon Fry is the college pastor at Messiah College in Mechanicsburg, Pennsylvania.

2. "Turn It Off" is recorded on the album *No Grey Lines*, by Mouthpi3ce, December 21, 2010, Format MP3.

3. Androzzo, Alma Bazel. *If I Can Help Somebody*. 1945. Publisher: Bossey and Hawkes, 1957.

4. Chris Chase, "Child Makes Heartwarming Request So He Can Push Disabled Brother in a 5K," *USA Today*, September 27, 2013, ftw.usatoday.com. Accessed August 4, 2014.

5. Jeffery D. Jones, *Practices in the Disciple-Forming Community* (Herndon, VA: Alban Institute, March 24, 2008, Number 192). This Alban Newsletter article is found

on www.transformingchurch.com Resource Toolbox.

6. Shane Claiborne, *The Irresistible Revolution: Living as an Ordinary Radical* (Grand Rapids: Zondervan, 2006).

7. Adam Taylor, *Mobilizing Hope: Faith-Inspired Activism for a Post-Civil Rights Generation* (Downers Grove, IL: IVP, 2010).

8. Deena Guzder, *Divine Rebels: American Christian Activists for Social Justice* (Chicago: Lawrence Hill, 2011).

9. Martin Luther King Jr., "The Drum Major Instinct," in Clayborne Carson and Peter Holloran, eds., *A Knock at Midnight: Inspiration from Great Sermons of Reverend Martin Luther King, Jr.* (New York: Warner, 1998).

CHAPTER 1

Christian Spirituality Basics

But you shall receive power (ability, efficiency, and might)
when the Holy Spirit has come upon you, and you shall
be My witnesses in Jerusalem and all Judea and Samaria
and to the ends (the very bounds) of the earth.

—Acts 1:8, AMP

Living lives of significance is a spiritual discipline set forth by Jesus in Acts 1:8. When we practice significance in our daily lives as a spiritual discipline, then, as Lee B. Spitzer, executive minister of American Baptist Churches of New Jersey, says, "our personal lives and our public witness are made one."[1] This happens as we choose to be witnesses to God's work in the world. Jesus uses a very direct word to tell his disciples how they are to live. He says, "And you *shall be*. . . ." "Shall be" indicates a matter of God's will and the disciples' state of obedient presence. As a disciple of Jesus, I have chosen to be present as is God's will for my life, an embodiment of the gospel. Wherever I am, the gospel is. Perhaps that is why the Greek word translated "witness" actually points to the word *martyr*. But in this sense it means that we bring our testimonies wherever we go. We lay down our testimonies to ourselves and pick up our testimonies as followers of Christ, to matters of forgiveness, love, righteousness and justice, peace, generosity, mercy, and grace. This is significance.

Acts 1:8 provides Jesus' model for our involvement in our surroundings and our world as witnesses. He tells his disciples how close to home and how far away our significance should reach. As witnesses, an active and not a passive role, we are instructed by Jesus to receive the power of the Holy Spirit, who will support and compel us to go. A diagram of this model, which I call the "Acts 1:8 Spheres of Significance," appears in figure 1.1.

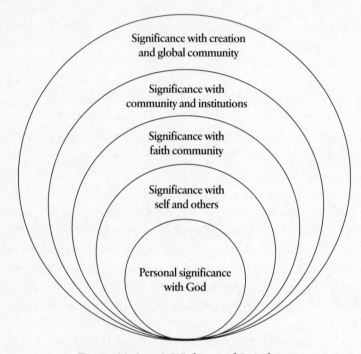

Figure 1.1. Acts 1:8 Spheres of Significance

A Close Look at the Spheres

According to Merriam-Webster, a sphere is "an area or range over or within which someone or something acts, exists, or has influence or significance."[2] Acts 1:8 seems to be appropriating this sense of sphere as a range of the believer's influence or significance in relating to the world as witnesses. In Jesus' final charge to his disciples before his ascension, he told them to live with significance within every sphere they would find themselves in at any given time. I have termed these "the five spheres of significance":

1st sphere–Personal significance with God
2nd sphere–Significance with self and others
3rd sphere–Significance with faith community
4th sphere–Significance with community and institutions
5th sphere–Significance with creation and global community

I will relate further applications of these spheres of significance in upcoming chapters as we see in the lives of biblical examples and others their significant reach and impact.

So what, then, is the answer for us as we reflect on our own significance in the sea of cultural indicators of who and what matters—that is, computer mediated relationships, culture-saturated sound bites, job titles, degrees, positions held, group membership, income, financial status, connectedness, family, friends, and face-to-face interactions? Wherein does our daily discipleship lead us to a spirituality that works with and far beyond or exclusive of either or any of these things that are perceived more as indicators of importance not of significance or meaning?

Evelyn Underhill, a twentieth-century theologian and mystic, wrote:

> For a spiritual life is simply a life in which all that we do comes from the centre, where we are anchored in God: a life soaked through and through by a sense of His reality and claim, and self-given to the great movement of His will.
>
> Most of our conflicts and difficulties come from trying to deal with the spiritual and practical aspects of our life separately instead of realizing them as parts of one whole. If our practical life is centreed on our own interests, cluttered up by possessions,

distracted by ambitions, passions, wants and worries, beset by a sense of our own rights and importance, or anxieties for our own future, or longings for our own success, we need not expect that our spiritual life will be a contrast to all this. The soul's house is not built on such a convenient plan: there are few soundproof partitions in it. Only when the conviction—not merely the idea—that the demand of the Spirit, however inconvenient, comes first and IS first rules the whole of it, will those objectionable noises die down which have a way of penetrating into the nicely furnished little oratory, and drowning all the quieter voices by their din.[3]

The life we live through our church missions and ministries is also the life we live through our work and our service every day regardless of titles, degrees, positions held, group memberships, income or financial status—or perhaps even because of those things. Living undivided and integrated lives where all we do is an expression of our faith is our spiritual discipline. Suffice it to say that there are many ways to think of Christian spirituality and many identities that are expressed as Christian spirituality. But fundamental and central to any spirituality that could be considered Christian would be to have its origin in the scriptural workings of the Spirit of God in both the Old and New Testaments. In the Old Testament we find the presence of God's Spirit as wind, breath, or spirit in the Hebrew word *ruah*, such as in Ezekiel 36:26-28: "I will give you a new heart and put a new spirit (*ruah*) in you; I will remove from you your heart of stone and give you a heart of flesh. And I will put my Spirit in you and move you to follow my decrees and be careful to keep my laws. Then you will live in the land I gave your ancestors; you will be my people, and I will be your God."

The Greek word *pneuma*, meaning "wind," "breath," and also "spirit," is used in reference to God's Spirit in the New Testament; for example, "For those who are led by the Spirit of God are the children of God" (Romans 8:14), and "But you will receive power when the Holy

Spirit comes on you; and you will be my witnesses in Jerusalem, and in all Judea and Samaria, and to the ends of the earth" (Acts 1:8).

Of course there are hundreds of uses of both *ruah* and *pneuma* in the Bible referring to wind, breath, and spirit, identifying God's character, works, presence, and/or movement.

As Christians our spirituality is rooted in the character and work of God in the world and is motivated by God's Spirit in us to live lives that fulfill God's purposes in our surroundings. One thing we see throughout Scripture is God's model for the presence and activity of God's people in the world. God is present. God is engaged. God is active. This is a path for us based in God's example; we are to be filled with the Spirit of God who empowers us to be, like God, present, engaged, and active personally.

Connections with Modern Models

We can see through the examples of five twentieth-century models spirituality that was present, active, and engaged. We will look at Dietrich Bonhoeffer's important contributions to the connection between community and spiritual discipline, Dorothy Day's devotion to and love of Scripture coupled with her love for people, Fannie Lou Hamer's fusion of prayer and purpose, Martin Luther King Jr.'s blend of study and service, and Jitsuo Morikawa's prioritization of faith and inclusiveness.

Model of Community and Spiritual Discipline

> Who stands firm? Only the one for whom the final standard is not his reason, his principles, his conscience, his freedom, his virtue, but who is ready to sacrifice all these, when in faith and sole allegiance to God he is called to obedient and responsible action: the responsible person, whose life will be nothing but an answer to God's question and call. —Dietrich Bonhoeffer[4]

Dietrich Bonhoeffer, pastor, theologian, activist, and martyr, felt his call from God during the time of Nazi Germany under Adolf Hitler.

5

His work was both chosen and what chose him. Educated at Union Seminary in New York, Bonhoeffer, after accepting a teaching position in America, was compelled to return to Germany to fight the political injustice and persecution being inflicted on the Jewish people in Germany.

An educator, Bonhoeffer established an underground seminary to teach Christian leaders. This became the community that he writes about in his book *Life Together: The Classic Exploration of Christian Community*. This and his writings on ethics available in a book he did not complete, *Ethics*, combined with other writings, give an informative and formative look into the measures that Christian discipleship will take to live into God's will for the world and our will for God's purposes. Bonhoeffer saw community closeness among Christians as God's blessing. He said of Christian community that "it is not to be taken for granted that the Christian has the privilege of living among other Christians."[5] Bonhoeffer cited Martin Luther's observation that Jesus set us an example by living not only among his disciples but among his enemies as well. The Christian life is lived in community, yes, but not isolated and cloistered, tucked away. Bonhoeffer, while living and teaching in the underground seminary, was a leader in the Confessing Church, the true Christian church in the presence of the Nazi regime.

Of particular interest closely related to this writing, Bonhoeffer offered counsel on spiritual disciplines to be practiced in community and personally by persons who are alone yet not alone. Specifically in the book *Life Together*, he discussed the need for communal prayer, singing together, the reading of Scripture in community, and meditation on Scripture done privately, saying that "God Himself requires them of us . . . we are performing a service that belongs to God."[6]

Bonhoeffer pointed to the question "Who will stand firm?" when we are challenged by the circumstances and situations that persist in the world, as we live among the good and the bad. The responsible person who stands firm is the one whose life is nothing but an answer to God's question and is willing to sacrifice his or her life as God calls. It was Bonhoeffer's faith, his call, and his ethic that motivated him to help Jewish persons in Germany to safety, to stand against the Hitler regime, and to found an underground seminary and teach Christians, ultimately costing him his life. This was the cost of his discipleship.

Model of Scripture and People

Dorothy Day was born in Brooklyn, New York, in 1897. As a child she lived in Oakland, California, and later in Chicago. Dorothy began her career as a journalist who reported on what was happening in society—poverty, wars, class struggle, the nuclear threat, and the civil rights movement. Day saw how these events impacted people economically, physically, and spiritually.[7] Influenced by her friendship with Peter Maurin, a visionary leader for actual engagement in Catholic social teaching, Day experienced a conversion to the Catholic faith and began to live by Catholic social teaching. Personally, she was particularly adhering to the gospel teaching from Matthew 25:35-45. Her passion is conveyed in her book *The Long Loneliness*: "There [at the national shrine of the Immaculate Conception in Washington, DC] I offered up a special prayer, a prayer which came with tears and with anguish, that some way would open up for me to use what talents I possessed for my fellow workers, for the poor."[8]

Day was led by her deep devotion to and unwavering love of Scripture coupled with her love for people. These are just three of the characteristics that make her ministry a witness of her understanding of what has been termed *personalism*.[9] Personalism is having respect for persons and honoring them for who they are, creatures of God, and not for anything else they may do to be considered as having value. They are valued for being unique and created in God's image.

Day was not just an observer of others' experiences but lived in dire circumstances herself. Although born into a middle-class family, as an adult she lived in poverty. She was engaged in her community hands on, participating in hunger strikes, reporting on bread riots, protesting on behalf of the poor, advocating for women's rights, and even being jailed—all while she was living out her spiritual practices of Scripture reading and prayer. Catholic social teachings became Day's guiding light to lead her as she lived her life in response to her faith.

Before there was a Catholic Worker Movement, there was the *Catholic Worker* newspaper, which began circulating during the Depression and was given this name because many Catholics were poor and the name served to influence Catholics, "who were criticized for a lack of social and political morality."[10] The success of the newspaper led to more people volunteering to help with the circulation. As more people became involved, others showed up with clothing, food, and other provisions. Soon thereafter, housing, becoming known as the Catholic Worker House, was provided for persons who were working with the paper; later Catholic Worker farms were established to aid in providing produce and food. Catholic Worker houses spread to other cities across the country and exist today for the purpose of helping the poor and fighting inequities. One such house is located in my hometown, Milwaukee, Wisconsin. It is called the Casa Maria Catholic Worker House. The Catholic Worker Movement is grounded in a firm belief in the God-given dignity of every human person. Today 227 Catholic Worker communities remain committed to nonviolence, voluntary poverty, prayer, and hospitality for the homeless, exiled, hungry, and forsaken. Catholic Workers continue to protest injustice, war, racism, and violence of all forms.[11]

Model of Prayer and Purpose

Fannie Lou Hamer's practice of prayer and purpose is an inspiring model for those seeking to live out their spirituality by bringing significance to their lives and to the lives of others. Mrs. Hamer was engaged as a church woman in the tumultuous fight for voting rights in Mississippi. The youngest child of a family of twenty children born in the Mississippi Delta and raised as Baptists, she was steeped in the Bible.

Hamer was gripped by her understanding of God's righteousness, encouraged by her belief that "God is on our side," and sustained by prayer and the singing of hymns. Hamer became known as "the lady who sings the hymns." Her favorites were "This Little Light of Mine" and "Go Tell It on the Mountain". Kay Mills, in her book "This Little Light of Mine", comments that "the hymns also reflected Hamer's belief that the civil rights struggle was a deeply spiritual one."[12] She strongly believed that no matter what would come to those facing the hatred and meanness from those opposing voting and civil rights, God would take care of them.

This combination of faith and action may not have been unusual, but the work that it took her to was. Her strength through prayer was evident in one critical moment when she met with then Senator Hubert Humphrey and challenged him to do the right thing without the fear of losing his job. She said to him, "Now if you lose this job of vice president [he was campaigning at the time] because you do what is right, because you help the MFDP [Mississippi Freedom Democratic Party cofounded by Hamer], everything will be all right. God will take care of you. But if you take the nomination this way [without dealing with the issues of voting rights, segregation, and equality], why, you will never be able to do any good for civil rights, for poor people, for peace, or any of those things you talk about. Senator Humphrey, I'm going to pray to Jesus for you."[13]

Fannie Lou Hamer touched God's creation in a personal way through her blend of prayer and purpose to accomplish God's purpose in the world. She is famously noted as having first said, "I am sick and tired of being sick and tired."[14] Perhaps this soul fatigue is the condition that can help us recognize God's call for us today. "You can pray until you faint, but unless you get up and try to do something, God is not going to put it in your lap,"[15] she said. Fannie Lou Hamer practiced what she prayed.

Model of Study and Service
Certainly Martin Luther King Jr. set forth a model of study and service. A lifelong learner, King, after having attended Morehouse College and

studying sociology, graduated from Crozer Theological Seminary with a BA in divinity and then a PhD in systematic theology from Boston University. He studied the social gospel of Walter Rauschenbusch and Reinhold Niebuhr and the theology of Paul Tillich. He embraced the methods of Mohandas Gandhi after having learned about the leadership he was providing in India. King continued his reading and learning well beyond his formal education throughout the civil rights movement.

A brilliant student, well-studied, and holding the highest degree credentials, Dr. King, according to Samuel DeWitt Proctor, preacher, pastor, educator, and civil rights leader, was reading Paul Tillich's *The Courage to Be* the night before he was to address the rally in Memphis, Tennessee—the night before he was killed.[16] King, with his impeccable credentials, stated that when he died and people spoke of what was significant about his life, he wanted them to say not that he had these credentials and more, but in short, that he was a servant. He lived to fulfill God's purpose in the world. Dr. King said in "The Drum Major Instinct" sermon that he would want it said that he tried to live his life serving others.

Dr. King's life is a model of spiritual activism faithfully lived to the fullest extent of the call of Acts 1:8, to the point of martyrdom. For a majority of us, "martyrdom" will be realized in our giving up our lives as living sacrifices to be used for Christ's sake, to live as the hands and feet of Christ in the earth. Dr. King's direct and outward expression of his spirituality was shown through his living the gospel call through his activism and his prophetic voice. He was compelled to relate and respond to the conditions of others, and that is how he received his soul identification, his significance—from being in relationship with others.

The ministry of social and moral justice was at the core of King's soul. This was not simply professional work or civic-minded service; this was soul work. For him to have done something else with his life would have meant living without being in alignment with his soul identification, which gave him his significance. I believe that King's lack of concern for his own life, understanding that he was at risk of being killed, was the result of his complete consummation by the will of God.

Model of Faith and Inclusiveness

Jitsuo Morikawa, a pastor, theologian, prophet, professor, denominational "bureaucrat," activist, and organizational leader, was marked by his spirit of faith and inclusiveness. While Morikawa was born of Buddhist parents in Hammond, British Columbia, he converted to Christianity at age sixteen.[17] Significant to his journey is the formative effect that his being denied missionary status because of his ancestry had. Without such status, along with his wife, Hazel, were placed in an internment camp during World War II while he served as an English-speaking pastor to three Japanese-American Baptist congregations in the Los Angeles area. During his internment Morikawa didn't stop ministering but served as a pastor at the internment camp in Poston, Arizona, for eighteen months.[18] Following his release from the internment camp in 1943, the Morikawas relocated to Chicago, where Jitsuo pastored a predominantly white congregation, leading to an influx of Japanese-Americans who were also released from detainment.[19]

For Morikawa, a saving relationship with Jesus Christ involved both faith and a commitment to justice that was expressed in Christ's inclusiveness. A most appealing aspect of Morikawa's service was given to the belief of the work or ministry of all persons—laity in ministry in their workplace. This inclusive theological position of Morikawa led him to become a leader in training laypersons to understand that what they do in their workplace is as much a response to God's call as that of anyone who serves as clergy. He emphasized the whole ministry of the people of God—the ministry of all persons.

Richard Broholm, a coworker with Morikawa, expressed Morikawa's belief in the ministry of all persons this way:

> For a man who spent his whole professional career in the institutional church, Jitsuo Morikawa had a passionate concern for

the world. And while his ministry took expression as a pastor and, in his words, as a "church bureaucrat," his commitment was to recover the whole ministry of all the people of God; to declare that for most laypersons the locus of their ministry is their daily work. . . . Further, he believed deeply that American Baptists had a unique contribution to make in empowering the laity for ministry.[20]

Just before he died in 1985, Morikawa wrote:

Because of our [American Baptist Churches, USA] smallness and hence flexibility, we have less to lose. We should identify a "driving force"; a singular, unique, most urgently needed missionary-evangelistic spear point around which our total resources be focused. That spear point or driving force in my judgment is the ministry of the laity in the institutions of our society. It should be informed by a theology of institutional accountability, to transform institutions to fulfill their true vocation and calling, namely, to serve the common good. There is no question that this is the urgent, most critical mission of the Church today and in the years ahead.[21]

Morikawa accomplished this belief of an inclusive call to ministry by establishing the Metropolitan Associates of Philadelphia (MAP). The stated purpose of MAP was to engage in experimental missionary action for the sake of a common witness to and participation in Christ's work of renewal in the city. Morikawa believed that persons' faith in Jesus Christ enlists them in the ministry of the gospel to serve in the institutions, businesses, schools, public squares, and marketplaces of their everyday lives. With this inclusive model, he sought to equip the saints for the full work of the church, building up the body of Christ in all places by all persons at all times. Morikawa summed up this point very powerfully:

If humankind is called to affect history and the reshaping of the world, then men and women in the business, political, social, health, educational and physical planning must see themselves under the mandate of calling; a calling to corporate responsibility. This means that every institution is confronted with the pressing question, "To what end?" To what purpose do we produce chemicals, educate children, build highways, elect officials, administer medicine, and provide social services?[22]

Challenges and Opportunities for the Local Church

The practice of spirituality that tends to be most prevalent in the church is one that focuses on personal and individual expressions of spirituality. This tendency to assume that spirituality is private and individual may move persons to be more self-serving, introverted, and isolated. The main spiritual practices employed may be those that Richard Foster identifies as the inward disciplines in his book *Celebration of Discipline: The Path to Spiritual Growth*[23] and that Brian McLaren notes as the seven ancient spiritual practices of the Abrahamic faith traditions (Judaism, Christianity, and Islam) in his book *Finding Our Way Again: The Return of the Ancient Practices*.[24]

Womanist theologian and social ethicist Emilie M. Townes brings the perspective of womanist theology to the forefront in spiritual practice and social witness in her book *In a Blaze of Glory: Womanist Spirituality as Social Witness*. She asserts that womanist spirituality grows out of individual and communal reflection on African American faith and life. She explains that spirituality is not grounded in the notion that spirituality is a force, a practice separate from who we are moment by moment. It is the deep kneading of humanity and divinity in one breath, one hope, and one vision.[25]

We tend to encourage prayer, study, solitude, meditation, fasting, Sabbath keeping, and worship by practicing them in a personal form of spirituality. Striking a balance with the outward spiritual disciplines as put forth by Foster would tend to lead to a more communal, collective, and integrated form of spirituality and spiritual practice that seeks to be engaged, active, and proactive. Herein is a challenge for the church today: *The church is called to be the presence of Christ among people in community and in relationship with others.* Being in relationship—in community—is God's desire for God's people. "You are the light of the world. A town built on a hill cannot be hidden. Neither do people light a lamp and put it under a bowl. Instead they put it on its stand, and it gives light to everyone in the house. In the same way, let your light shine before others, that they may see your good deeds and glorify your Father in heaven" (Matthew 5:14-16).

Spirituality that works will guide persons in service that not only leads to living lives of significance but also in discovering the fulfillment of their discipleship and their unique calling by God. Many churches underemphasize spirituality in the Christian's life and calling. We must highlight vocation and calling within discipleship ministry.

As disciples of Christ, we each are given a unique place in the ministry of Christ that works to fulfill God's purpose in the world. All of us are called for some purpose. This calling is established in Jeremiah 29:11: "For I know the plans I have for you," declares the LORD, "plans to prosper you and not to harm you, plans to give you hope and a future." While this text is written to Israel during their time of exile, it can be taken as a promise by all believers. Further, God's calling of people is seen throughout the Bible in characters such as Moses, Jeremiah, and Mary.

More recent developments of emphasizing *calling* in colleges and universities has come from the Lilly Endowment programs for the theological exploration of vocation. Major funding began in 2001. The Fund for Theological Education and other groups have begun preparing persons to respond to their calls as well. Over the past ten years, the culture of call within denominational bodies has been a growing ministry focus, particularly to engage emerging leaders and the younger generation. Local churches are beginning to give attention to creating a ministry strategy to emphasize and develop a culture of call in the church, but resources to do so are scarce. By and large this effort has yet to make a significant stride to strategically educate and encourage calling and vocation as a vital church discipleship ministry.

Recently, as I managed university programs in ministry formation for undergraduates discerning their call to professional church ministry, I was surprised to hear from some pastors that they had not sufficiently educated their young people to consider matters of their calling, particularly a calling to a life in ministry—lay or ordained. These pastors, however, did express a strong interest in supporting the development of an educational approach to vocation and calling as a part of their discipleship ministries, but they were without the adequate resources to do so. This is a challenge for many churches.

Opportunities for Local Church Ministries

Twenty-first-century culture is being understood and adapted to by the church. Many churches are undergoing what is known as "adaptive change" processes. Adaptive change is a metaphor used to describe the journey the church is currently engaged in in an attempt to meet the challenges and the opportunities of the changing culture. Alan Roxburgh addresses the subject in an article titled "Moneyball—Adaptive Change at the Movies" for the Missional Church Network:[26] "We believe the language and practice of adaptive change provides a helpful set of tools for asking the questions of what God might be up to just now. We stress that adaptive change is a tool and not the answer; it is, however, a very helpful tool for journeying in a new land where most of our current skill sets don't work and existing solutions keep taking us back to the same old places." While the purpose of this writing is not to address the work of adaptive change, it is helpful to understand the concept as we look at the challenges and opportunities facing the local church.

Challenges and opportunities of our culture provide the environment from which what I previously discussed emerges, such as social networking, texting and tweeting, and fast-paced living. What also emerges is a generation of "nones," identified in the Pew Forum on Religion and Public Life Report *"Nones" on the Rise* as a growing number of Americans who identify themselves as not religiously affiliated.[27] Certainly the culture is producing an increasing number of people who do not attend church services regularly and who seek to have their spiritual needs met through nonchurch activity. Our times create the human thirst for deeper experiences, for finding meaning and connection between *who* we are and *what* we do.

Clearly people are not looking to do more, to be busier, or to become more occupied. They are not looking for ways just to be more important. They are seeking deeper meaning through purposeful, faithful engagement in life whereby their spirituality is expressed through whatever they do—work, play, love, give, live.

This points us toward opportunities that are open to the church. In many ways, fulfilling our spiritual significance by connecting with God's purpose in the earth can bring a far better sense of fulfillment that can give a weary spirit rest and restfulness than does living without a larger spiritual purpose. Jesus invites us to this way of life by saying, "Come to me, all you who are weary and burdened, and I will give you rest. Take my yoke upon you and learn from me, for I am gentle and humble in heart, and you will find rest for your souls. For my yoke is easy and my burden is light" (Matthew 11:28-30). *The Message* renders this text in a much more pronounced way: "Are you tired? Worn out? Burned out on religion? Come to me. Get away with me and you'll recover your life. I'll show you how to take a real rest. Walk with me and work with me— watch how I do it. Learn the unforced rhythms of grace. I won't lay anything heavy or ill-fitting on you. Keep company with me and you'll learn to live freely and lightly."

Learn the unforced rhythms of grace. The local church now has an opportunity to guide persons into a rhythm of grace that makes for a more life-giving pace in our lives and gives greater inner peace, deeper fulfillment, and joy because we are discovering the significance in our lives that comes through being in the company of Jesus, walking with him, working with him, and living as him to bring God's kingdom here on earth.

Another great opportunity for the church in this twenty-first century is to engage with the spiritual activism and social activism characteristic of the millennial generation, also known as the echo boomers, the eighteen- to thirty-five-year-olds, those born between 1978 and 1995. Their traits and characteristics have been well-studied. Millennials are reported to make up 27.4 percent of the US population according to the US Census Bureau data.[28] Here are just some of the known factors about this specific generation. Millennials surveyed about what the most important things in their lives are said:

- Helping others in need (21 percent)
- Being a good parent (52 percent)
- Having a successful marriage (30 percent)
- Owning a home (20 percent)
- Having lots of free time (9 percent)
- Living a very religious life (15 percent)
- Having a high paying job (15 percent)

It is informative here to note that religion ranks lower in importance for Millenials—fifteen percent. Twenty-eight percent say living a very religious life is very important but not one of the most important goals for them. Strikingly about twenty-six percent say this is not important to them at all.[29]

This generation was groomed to achieve and excel. They are entrepreneurial hard workers who thrive on flexibility. They were born with technology in hand, always knowing the laptop computer, Internet, portable music devices, CDs, DVDs, and video games. They are the technology settlers in a tech world pioneered by the baby boomers. Millennials are understood to be most socially conscious, most education-minded, upbeat, and full of self-esteem. Most importantly they are very high in volunteerism.[30]

Millennials have been educated to be socially engaged through experiential learning in their schools through service learning, externships, and local and international service immersion programs. Some have given service to communities through the governmental-sponsored AmeriCorps program. This generation can be best engaged through ministry and discipleship approaches that help them prepare for their future and ours; bring out their gifts, callings, and strengths; and engage them in the affairs of their communities, country, and world.

The significance of living as the church in our day is where discipleship comes alive and thrives. Living a spirituality that works brings significance to our lives, which not only fulfills God's call to us, but in turn helps us to fulfill God's purpose in the world. Servant leadership is one such movement in this century (it actually began in the twentieth century) that connects spirituality, action, and the spirit of serving others. Christians who embrace the tenets of servant leadership are able to see their aspirations of living the gospel call in what they do as servant leaders. This kind of lived spirituality gives direction and purpose to people's lives.

The Modern Servant Leadership Movement

Jitsuo Morikawa was a central leader in the lay-work ministry movement, the ministry of the whole people of God with clergy acting as "pastors to a servant people" serving in institutions and workplaces. Richard Broholm assisted Morikawa, who both served in leadership of the American Baptist Home Mission Society in the 1970s and then went on to start the Metropolitan Associates of Philadelphia. Following this work, Broholm started a program at Andover Newton Theological Seminary for training laity in the workplace. Here is where he met Robert Greenleaf and helped to establish the Greenleaf Center for Servant Leadership.

Robert Greenleaf, a nonchurchman and former AT&T professional inspired by the work of Morikawa and Broholm, began a new movement called servant leadership. Greenleaf described the servant leader in this way: "The servant-leader is servant first. It begins with the natural feeling that one wants to serve. Then conscious choice brings one to aspire to lead."[31]

The ten identified characteristics of the servant leader are these:

1. Listening to others
2. Empathizing with others
3. Leading others into wholeness
4. Persuading others in the hope of achieving consensus
5. Having awareness of self, others, and issues
6. Showing foresight
7. Conceptualizing and visioning
8. Committing to the growth of others
9. Demonstrating stewardship
10. Building community within groups[32]

The servant leadership movement has influenced business, institutions, organizations, and churches. The ultimate model of servant leadership is Jesus Christ. When I attended my first servant leadership conference a few years ago, I was surprised to note the central references to faith and the model of Jesus, and to hear many people expressing how this practice gives them opportunity to live their faith within their organizational and work lives. I overheard participants saying that being a servant leader helps them to help others achieve their full capacity and aspirations, to help their businesses work for the greater good, and to be authentic in their workplaces.

An outgrowth of this movement is the emergence of service learning through experiential learning programs in high schools and colleges. When I began working at Cardinal Stritch University in Milwaukee twenty-five years ago, service-learning programs were just being introduced as pedagogy for faculty, but for campus ministries it was a way to engage students in learning about serving through acts of advocacy, civic and nonprofit activism, and social justice. Service-learning programs are very popular among millennials and younger emerging generations, resulting in a more service-sensitive future leadership.

Spirituality paired with a strong sense of service is key in living out a vital spirit and performing vital service. Understanding such spirituality is important to disciple making. The next chapter explores this further.

Notes

1. Lee B. Spitzer, *Making Friends, Making Disciples: Growing Your Church through Authentic Relationships*, Living Church Series, Dwight J. Stinnett, ed. (Valley Forge, PA: Judson, 2010), xiv.

2. *Merriam-Webster's Collegiate Dictionary*, s.v. "sphere," 11th ed. (Springfield, MA: Merriam-Webster, 2003).

3. Evelyn Underhill, *The Spiritual Life* (Harrisburg, PA: Morehouse, 1984), 32–34.

4. Dietrich Bonhoeffer, "After Ten Years," *Letters and Papers from Prison*, enl. ed. (New York: Macmillan, 1971), 5.

5. Dietrich Bonhoeffer, *Life Together: The Classic Exploration of Christian Community* (New York: Harper and Row, 1954), 121.

6. Ibid., 122.

7. James Allaire and Rosemary Broughton, *Praying with Dorothy Day (Companions for the Journey)* (Winona, MN: Saint Mary's Press, 1995), 127.

8. Dorothy Day, *The Long Loneliness* (San Francisco: Harper, 1952), 284.

9. Allaire and Broughton, *Praying with Dorothy Day*, 127.

10. Ibid.

11. Go to www.catholicworker.org for more information.

12. Kay Mills, *This Little Light of Mine: The Life of Fannie Lou Hamer (Civil Rights and the Struggle for Black Equality in the Twentieth Century)* (Lexington: University Press of Kentucky, 2007), xxii.

13. Ibid.

14. Kay Mills, *This Little Light of Mine*, 93, cites Jerry DeMuth, "Fannie Lou Hamer: Tired of Being Sick and Tired," *The Nation*.

15. Charles Marsh, *God's Long Summer: Stories of Faith and Civil Rights*, Chapter One: *"I'm on My Way, Praise God": Mrs. Hamer's Fight for Freedom*. Online book. www.washingtonpost.com/wp-srv/style/longterm/.../godslongsummer.htm.

16. This information was obtained from an interview with Samuel Proctor contained in this video: William D. Watley, *Roots of Resistance: The Nonviolent Ethic of Martin Luther King, Jr.*, (Valley Forge, PA: Judson, 1985).

17. Kenan Heise, "Rev. Jitsuo Morikawa, Baptist Leader," *Chicago Tribune*, July 23, 1987, http://articles.chicagotribune.com/1987-07-23/news/8702230844_1_baptist-leader-american-baptist-churches-usa-southern-baptist-theological-seminary.

18. Ibid.

19. Go to http://chsmedia.org and search for Jitsuo Morikawa or First Baptist Church of Chicago Records, 1834–1983.

20. Richard Broholm, "Trustees of the Universe: Recovering the Whole Ministry of the People of God" (Seeing Things Whole, Inc., 2001), 22, http://www.seeingthingsw hole.org/uploads/STW-Trustee-of-the-Universe_567684.pdf.

21. Ibid.

22. David Specht with Richard Broholm, "Toward a Theology of Institutions," The Greenleaf Center for Servant-Leadership and Seeing Things Whole, 5, http://www.seeingthingswhole.org/uploads/STW-toward-theology-of-institu-tions_279644.pdf.

23. Richard J. Foster, *Celebration of Discipline: The Path to Spiritual Growth* (San Francisco: HarperSanFrancisco, 1988).

24. Brian McLaren, *Finding Our Way Again: The Return of the Ancient Practices* (Nashville: Thomas Nelson, 2008).

25. Emilie M. Townes, *In a Blaze of Glory: Womanist Spirituality as Social Witness* (Nashville: Abingdon, 1995), 160.

26. Alan Roxburgh, "Moneyball–Adaptive Change at the Movies," The Missional Network. www.the missionalnetwork.com>Resources>Articles>Leadership.

27. Sharon Stencel, ed., *"Nones" on the Rise: One-in-Five Adults Have No Religious Affiliation* (Washington, DC: Pew Research Center, 2012), 77.

28. United States Census Bureau, "2010 Census Briefs–Age and Sex Composition: 2010, Table 1 (2011)".

29. "Millennials: Confident. Connected. Open to Change," Chapter 3: Identity, Priorities, and Outlook, February, 2010, 18. Pew Research Center www.pewresearch-center.org/millennials.

30. Paul Taylor and Scott Keeter, eds., *Millennials: Confident. Connected. Open to Change* (Washington, DC: Pew Research Center, 2010), 113.

31. Larry C. Spears, "The Understanding and Practice of Servant-Leadership," in *Practicing Servant Leadership*, ed. Larry C. Spears and Michele Lawrence (San Francisco: Jossey-Bass, 2004), 9.

32. Larry C. Spears and John C. Burkhardt, "Servant Leadership and Philanthropic Institutions," in Spears and Lawrence, eds., *Practicing Servant Leadership*, 72–73.

CHAPTER 2

What Is This Spirituality?

> But [GOD's] already made it plain how to live, what to do,
> what GOD is looking for in men and women. It's quite
> simple: Do what is fair and just to your neighbor, be com-
> passionate and loyal in your love, and don't take yourself
> too seriously—take God seriously.
>
> —Micah 6:6-8, MSG

"Do what is fair and just to your neighbor, be compassionate and loyal
in your love, and don't take yourself too seriously—take God seriously."
These words are the first block in building a spirituality that works—a
spirituality that leads to a life of spiritual and personal significance as a
grace of God.

I have worked in the ministry of Christian disciple making and spirituality now for over thirty years. I started with very little knowledge of
Christian spirituality. During the early 1990s I began my own searching
for a deeper and more authentic relationship with God that would
enliven me on Thursday just as it did on Sunday. I was yearning for more
than what my regular church attendance and participation were giving
me. I came upon an abundance of writings on spirituality during this
time and read more and more. Then I began my doctoral studies in spirituality with a determination to understand the deeper applications that
spirituality as an approach to Christian living could give me for my own
growth and more so as God's call for my focus in ministry.

A Working Definition

My understanding of Christian spirituality has evolved over the years of walking with this ministry focus. Certainly there are many other definitions, but I define Christian spirituality as *experiencing the love of Jesus in every person in every situation at all times through the presence of the Holy Spirit; that love is expressed in our engaging the work that Jesus desires to have done at the leading of the Holy Spirit.* The result is our answering God's call in all aspects of our everyday lives with meaning and purpose to the glory of God.

This fourfold definition can be easily remembered as *experiencing, expressing, engaging every day.*

Experiencing the Love of Jesus

In actuality, significance does not begin with our doing. It starts with the moment we come to know and be embraced by God's love through the saving grace and sacrifice of God's Son, Jesus Christ, not only for our salvation but for our living. "I came that they may have life, and have it abundantly" says Jesus (John 10:10, NRSV). Abundantly? Yes, and that meets with significance.

Love Is Expressed

I love the song "I Give Myself Away" sung by William McDowell that talks about how he surrenders and gives himself to be used for God's purposes. Our readiness to surrender our lives to the love of God for the purposes of God *is* our love for God fully expressed as worship. Romans 12:1 says, "I urge you, brothers and sisters, in view of God's mercy, to offer your bodies as a living sacrifice, holy and pleasing to God—this is your true and proper worship." It is at this point of surrender and acceptance that we become ready for engagement.

Engaging the Work of Jesus

Our spirituality is lived through acts of engagement. Words that connect with *engage* are *pursue, employ, touch, absorb, engross,* and *enlist.* Together they paint a portrait of someone who is motivated by the causes of Christ pursuing that which makes visible the hands and feet of Christ. But we may ask the driving question, "What is that work of Jesus in our times?" Jesus' work is concerned with three things: salvation, justice, and righteousness. The work of salvation is done. It is a free gift to all who would believe on Jesus Christ as Lord and Savior. Ours is to share this good news through our witness, our worship, and our work.

The work of justice is caring for those who cannot do for themselves—those who do not have the ability, the means, or the capacity to pull themselves up from their circumstances in which they find themselves. In Jesus' day these vulnerable people were the widows, the orphans, and oftentimes strangers. In our times, the complexities of economies, geographies, social status, institutions, and even communities include those who are similarly situated as vulnerable and marginalized populations just as in Jesus' time. Consider who may be on your doorstep or in your path who is vulnerable or marginalized—children in poverty, victims of domestic violence, people who find themselves homeless, people with mental illness or physical disability, immigrants of varying documentation, the elderly and infirm, just to name a few.

Our engagement in the work of righteousness is our call to be "concerned about that which God is concerned about" and adjust our lives accordingly.[1] In this sense, righteousness captures our attention to things that are truly and deeply in God's heart.

Every Day to the Glory of God

The Christian life is lived every day. There are no days off, are there? So it is with living our spirituality—we are who we are day in and day out, and we live to the glory of God. We can experience significance in our lives as we are engaged in God's purpose for us in the world and God's plan for our living day to day. Important people in our culture generally have glory heaped on them for their status, their great contributions, notable performance, and achievements. That's fine. But we, on the other hand, even when receiving such accolades, must know that who we are and what we do are for the glory of God and to his praise every day.

Spirituality Undergirded by Scripture

Micah 6:6-8 undergirds this spirituality, calling for us to live in relationship with ourselves, with God, and with others. Attempting to live disengaged from others in isolation is a spiritual existence that is of no use. Spirituality must be lived in the context of culture, with culture meaning our ways of believing, behaving, and perceiving. Our times and our culture have great need. We live as Christ's hands and feet, led by the Holy Spirit, in great expectation that we might perform what is asked of us in the Micah text, "Do what is fair and just to your neighbor, be compassionate and loyal in your love" (6:8, MSG).

Practicing a spiritual life that exercises only the private and personal expressions of Christian living is nurturing to the individual, but it does not meet with our assignment from Scripture as demonstrated in Matthew 25:34-40:

> "The King will say to those on his right, 'Come, you who are blessed by my Father; take your inheritance, the kingdom prepared for you since the creation of the world. For I was hungry and you gave me something to eat, I was thirsty and you gave me something to drink, I was a stranger and you invited me in, I needed clothes and you clothed me, I was sick and you looked after me, I was in prison and you came to visit me.'
>
> "Then the righteous will answer him, 'Lord, when did we see you hungry and feed you, or thirsty and give you something to drink? When did we see you a stranger and invite you in, or needing clothes and clothe you? When did we see you sick or in prison and go to visit you?'

"The King will reply, 'Truly I tell you, whatever you did for one of the least of these brothers and sisters of mine, you did for me.'"

For disciples of Christ, the glory is all God's and the pleasure is all ours. We serve Christ as we serve one another. "Do what is fair and just to your neighbor, be compassionate and loyal in your love, and don't take yourself too seriously—take God seriously."

Spirituality in Tradition

This practice of spirituality leads us to engage the "inward disciplines," as defined by Richard Foster in the *Celebration of Discipline*, by taking seriously the "outward disciplines," and more specifically here, the discipline of service.[2] We see this also in "active spirituality," as described by Parker J. Palmer in *The Active Life: A Spirituality of Work, Creativity, and Caring*,[3] and even in the emergence of "missional spirituality" that is being explored through the missional church movement today and in the "womanist spirituality" as put forth in Emilie Townes's publication *Embracing the Spirit*.[4]

So what is spiritual discipline? As defined by Foster, spiritual disciplines are the "means of receiving God's grace. Disciplines allow us to place ourselves before God so God can transform us."[5] In other words, they place us in the path of God where growth, change, and maturity can happen. They have been noted as the *pathway to Christian maturity*.

Traditional spiritual disciplines as seen by Foster include practices such as prayer, study, service, solitude, meditation, fasting, submission, confession, worship, guidance, and celebration. These disciplines, also known as *exercises*, help to build us up in our inner lives in order to support growth in our actions and behaviors. These acts and behaviors connect with our communities' needs and God's purposes. In particular, in the pursuit for social justice, we can all do our part to make "justice roll down like a mighty stream." In this, prayer is action; study is preparation; service is engagement; solitude is renewal; meditation is reflection; fasting is focus; submission is commitment; confession is integrity; worship is gratitude; guidance is wisdom; and celebration is rejoicing, and I would add Sabbath is rest. The keeping of these inner disciplines stirs up, supports, and sustains us in our call to touch one of God's creations in a personal way.

A pastor told me an old story during my teen years about a man who had sustained a severe injury that left him with no arms. The village he lived in needed volunteers who would go to the well and pump water to bring to the village during a terrible time of need. All volunteers were welcome. When this man considered his physical challenge, he prayed and asked God what he could possibly do to help since he had no arms. The response he received was to go to the woman who was blind standing at the water pump ready to pump. She needed someone who could tell her when the bucket was full. His discipline to pray in all things resulted in his seeing a contribution he could make to meet the need of his community, which was to use his gift of sight to tell the woman when her bucket was full.

Joan Chittister, author and Catholic theologian, in addressing the relationship between culture and spirituality, says it is about "what you do with what you are and why you do it." Chittister also adds a perspective on the historical stream of spirituality, a stream that is a *performative* spirituality that is very action-centered. She says, "Performers in the spiritual life pray every day, 'Thy kingdom come, Thy will be done,' and then they do something to bring it. Performers are people who know that the Word is incomplete until it has become transforming action."[6]

However, in answering the question "What do our times and our culture need?" or the more specific question, "What is it that God wants done in the world?" we must own that we are the ones whom God has chosen to do it.

Notes

1. A definition of righteousness rendered by Dr. James E. Leary, former pastor of Calvary Baptist Church, in Milwaukee, Wisconsin.

2. Richard J. Foster, *Celebration of Discipline: The Path to Spiritual Growth*, rev. 1st ed. (San Francisco: Harper and Row, 1988), ix.

3. Parker J. Parker, *The Active Life: A Spirituality of Work, Creativity, and Caring* (San Francisco: Jossey-Bass, 1990).

4. Emilie M. Townes, ed., *Embracing the Spirit: Womanist Perspectives on Hope, Salvation, and Transformation*, Vol. 13 of the Bishop Henry McNeal Turner/Sojourner Truth series in Black religion (Maryknoll: Orbis Books, 1997).

5. Richard J. Foster, *Celebration of Discipline*), 7.

6. A transcript of a speech titled "Spirituality and Contemporary Culture II," delivered by Joan Chittister during the National Forum of the Center for Progressive Christianity held June 1–3, 2000, in Irvine, California. Accessed from www.religion-online.org/showarticle.asp?title=1651.

CHAPTER 3

Spirituality Present in Scripture

It is not until you have touched your finger to the flame
that you can know the real meaning of the candle. This is
how it is with sacred texts.

—Myoung Suk Ja[1]

For Christians the Bible is the source of spiritual examples, models, and
ancient records of God's interaction with and intention for God's creation, and it is our starting point for this exploration of spirituality. The
late seminary professor Barbara E. Bowe referred to Scripture as "a reser-
voir of 'living water' that mediates to us the divine presence," saying "it is
no wonder, then, that we should turn to this living word as the privileged
foundation of our life of faith, our spirituality for today."[2] Through the
Scriptures we can see that this spirituality rests within the workings of
God in the formation of central figures such as Abraham, Moses, Elijah,
Jeremiah, Esther, Lydia, Paul, and others then and now, but also in persons who were more peripheral but still critically instrumental to God's
plan such as Rahab, Huldah, Hannah, Mary Magdalene, and Barnabas.
All of these individuals (among many others) lived their spirituality per-
forming the work from God that they were inspired or directed to live.

We must own that we are the ones God has chosen to do what God
wants done in the world. Consistently throughout the Bible God's will
is fulfilled through people—and a time or two God uses a donkey, a
whale, a burning bush, a pillar of fire, or rain.

Biblical characters' expression of spirituality shows up in their relationship with God, the result of which is answering God's call in all aspects of their everyday lives with meaning and purpose for God's glory. We will look at some of these biblical characters, including Abraham and Sarah in the patriarchal/matriarchal period; at Deborah and Josiah during the period of the Judges and Kings; at numerous persons in the prophetic period, such as Huldah and Nehemiah; at Esther in the historical period; and at Jesus in the Gospels.

They Answered the Call of God

We can learn from the Old and New Testament personalities who set a path for us to also lead lives of biblical proportion, so to speak. Abraham, Sarah, Deborah, Josiah, Jeremiah, Micah, Esther, Lydia, and Paul were in their own times just ordinary people, which proves that God uses ordinary, everyday humanity, people like you and me. What is extraordinary is the way in which they were positioned to listen and move to the leading of God's call—God's desire for their lives for God's own purpose. They were propositioned in spirit by Spirit, in heart through Heart, in the contextual sets of circumstances occurring in community. These people help us to identify engaged spirituality. They show us a way, a life pattern.

The Way of the Patriarchs and Matriarchs

The patriarchal/matriarchal period in history begins in Genesis 12, where it is inaugurated with the call of Abram/Abraham, and extends into chapter 50. Patriarchal/matriarchal refer to the father/mother or founder of a race, family, or nation, and the father/mother is also generally the leader or ruler of the clan or nation. God promised Abraham that he would be made the father of many nations and that Sarah would bear him a son and be the mother of many nations (Genesis 17:4,16). Abraham, Sarah, and consequently their son, Isaac (wife Rebecca), and grandsons Jacob (wives Rachel and Leah and maidservants Bilhah and Zilpah) and Esau (wives who bore sons were Adah, Oholibamah, and Basemath), are the primary patriarchs/matriarchs during this period. Abraham had a son, Ishmael, from Sarah's slave girl, Hagar. Hagar was taken as a surrogate since to that point Sarah had no son (Genesis 16). But Sarah asked Abraham to send Hagar and Ishmael away after her son, Isaac, second son to Abraham, was born because of her concern about inheritance. Central to the political struggles and disputes historically are the two nations that result from the two sons of Abraham—Isaac, about whom Scripture says that through him Abraham's offspring "will be named for you" (Genesis 21:12, NRSV) and Ishmael, who Scripture says will be made into a nation also because he is Abraham's offspring too (Genesis 21:13). Covenants or promises of God were made to these ancestors of faith that are still being fulfilled in our time, and they are the genesis of struggles that continue in the Middle East through today.

How was it that this Abram was so positioned to perceive and recognize God's workings in his life? What was in this ordinary man's disposition that allowed him to hear God's voice in his spirit? What spiritual attunement was practiced by this patriarch?

Abram's father, Terah, was an idol worshiper. We can read for ourselves in Joshua 24:2 where God declared through Joshua, "Long ago your ancestors—Terah and his sons Abraham and Nahor—lived beyond the Euphrates and served other gods" (NRSV). Charles Spurgeon, in his sermon "Effectual Calling—Illustrated by the Call of Abram," offered this:

> "Yet the Sovereign Grace of God pitched upon the household of Terah, and out of that favored family the Lord of Hosts made a Divine selection of the person of Abram. Why, I say again, why, remains in the inscrutable Purposes of God. . . . Abram was a man with faults, [a] man also with many virtues . . . yes, but those virtues given to him by God's Spirit, and not the cause of his Election, but the result.[3]

With that being said, God graced Abram, a Hebrew, to have an attunement toward God and allowed him to hear God's Spirit tell him to move his family to a place he would be shown. From that point on, Abraham's spirituality was marked by faith and obedience lived out in the presence of God, family, and community. Not that his faith never wavered! Abraham, however, demonstrated that extraordinary faith, trust, and obedience to God's will are central to a spiritual life that pleases God. Genesis 15:6 (NRSV) records, "[Abram] believed the LORD, and the LORD reckoned it to him as righteousness." Further, Hebrews 11:8-12 (CEB) says of Abraham:

> By faith Abraham obeyed when he was called to go out to a place that he was going to receive as an inheritance. He went out without knowing where he was going. By faith he lived in the land he had been promised as a stranger. He lived in tents along with Isaac and Jacob, who were coheirs of the same promise. He was looking forward to a city that has foundations, whose architect and builder is God. By faith even Sarah received the ability to have a child, though she herself was barren and past the age for having children, because she believed that the one who promised was faithful. So descendants were born from one man (and he was as good as dead). They were as many as the number of the stars in the sky and as countless as the grains of sand on the seashore.

Perhaps a purpose for this calling of Abraham and the patriarchal descendants is more closely found in Genesis 18:19: "I have chosen him, so that he will direct his children and his household after him to keep the way of the LORD by doing what is right and just, so that the LORD will bring about for Abraham what he has promised him." So we see faith and obedience as foundations to spirituality. See figure 3.1 for Abraham's sphere of significance.

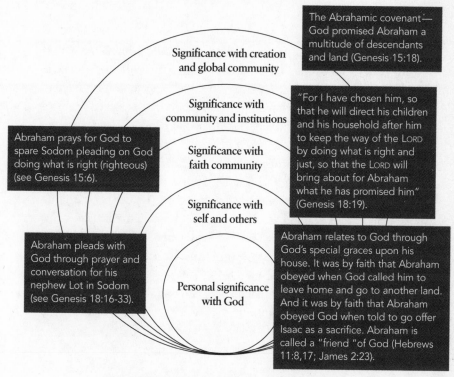

The Abrahamic covenant—God promised Abraham a multitude of descendants and land (Genesis 15:18).

"For I have chosen him, so that he will direct his children and his household after him to keep the way of the LORD by doing what is right and just, so that the LORD will bring about for Abraham what he has promised him" (Genesis 18:19).

Abraham prays for God to spare Sodom pleading on God doing what is right (righteous) (see Genesis 15:6).

Abraham pleads with God through prayer and conversation for his nephew Lot in Sodom (see Genesis 18:16-33).

Abraham relates to God through God's special graces upon his house. It was by faith that Abraham obeyed when God called him to leave home and go to another land. And it was by faith that Abraham obeyed God when told to go offer Isaac as a sacrifice. Abraham is called a "friend "of God (Hebrews 11:8,17; James 2:23).

Significance with creation and global community

Significance with community and institutions

Significance with faith community

Significance with self and others

Personal significance with God

Figure 3.1. Abraham's Sphere of Significance

The Way of Judges and Kings

The judges had a special spiritual role in the community and a unique place in the history of Israel. The judges were raised up by God to restore order or to right injustice in the days when Israel had no king but the Lord. When the community had an active judge, they did what was right in the sight of the Lord. When there was no judge, the people returned to doing what was right in their own eyes. This model of government endured for many years among God's people, predating the reigns of Saul, David, and Solomon, the only monarchs of united Israel.

Deborah

A prophet, the fourth judge, and a military leader prior to the start of the period of the Kings, Deborah is the only female judge mentioned in the Bible, which is quite a place to hold in Israelite history. We find Deborah in Judges 4:4 holding court under the so-called Palm of Deborah, delivering God's message to the people and settling disputes as a judge.

Apparently, in this vocation, gender was not an issue nor was it a hindrance to Deborah in her work and ministry.

Deborah exercised courage and calling based on her personal relationship with God and God's people, her people, the Israelites. She must have shown strong and competent practices of listening for God's voice and speaking truth to their problems. Notice Deborah's reach as demonstrated in the illustration below. What occurs for Deborah, as with others, is the result of maintaining her central circle from which all else flows—her relationship with God, which feeds and sustains her to be present and engaged.

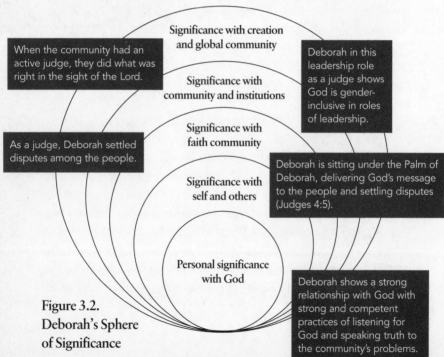

Significance with creation and global community

When the community had an active judge, they did what was right in the sight of the Lord.

Deborah in this leadership role as a judge shows God is gender-inclusive in roles of leadership.

Significance with community and institutions

Significance with faith community

As a judge, Deborah settled disputes among the people.

Deborah is sitting under the Palm of Deborah, delivering God's message to the people and settling disputes (Judges 4:5).

Significance with self and others

Personal significance with God

Deborah shows a strong relationship with God with strong and competent practices of listening for God and speaking truth to the community's problems.

Figure 3.2.
Deborah's Sphere
of Significance

Like Deborah, each of us, when living fully and authentically, can yield to God's will for our lives, giving us significance. Our spheres, or circles, are our natural contexts, communities, and cultures that we align with and are set within.

Josiah

Josiah was sovereign over the Southern Kingdom of Judah, long after the kingdom of David and Solomon became divided. Commonly thought of as the "boy king" because he was eight years old when he took the throne, Josiah reigned for thirty-one years. Following the tragic reigns of both his grandfather and father, Josiah was next in line to lead Jerusalem (2 Chronicles 33:25). Just as we saw that gender was not an issue in Deborah's leadership, for Josiah age was not an issue when it came to his taking the throne. As today's church and society research ways to engage the younger generation in our churches, organizations, and institutions, we may be challenged to transform our thinking about who God chooses to be next in line for leadership, particularly when we look at what God was able to accomplish through Josiah.

Josiah, following in the lineage of King David, was *the right person* for what God wanted to accomplish. It was significant enough that he came in a long line of kings and probably understood that one day that seat would be his. It is true that, were it not for the assassination of his father, Josiah would have had more years to prepare himself for such a task. But Josiah took his time to understand the situation. What had God been doing in Josiah's spirit during his childhood? What was his formation? We don't know the specifics, but we can see that God had a special hand on Josiah so that when he became sixteen, or "while he was still young, he began to seek the God of his father David. In his twelfth year [age twenty] he began to purge Judah and Jerusalem of high places, Asherah poles and idols" (2 Chronicles 34:3).

The opening commentary on Josiah in 2 Chronicles 34:2 says that he "did what was right in the eyes of the LORD and followed the ways of his father David, not turning to the right or to the left." This was in stark contrast to the legacy of his grandfather Manasseh and his father, Amon, of whom we read, they "did evil in the eyes of the LORD" (2 Chronicles 33:2;22). The affairs of Jerusalem, the spiritual life of the people, and the practice of religious tradition had suffered and diminished greatly during their reigns.

As the right person, however, Josiah not only wanted to follow the God of David himself, but he actively began restoring the community. As a result of his maturing spirituality, he made restoring Judah's religious heritage a signature focus of his leadership.

Josiah's significance cannot be understated, and he began his leadership role when he was eight years old. Having a heart to follow the God of David and preserve his spiritual heritage, he did what was his to do as a descendant of a good kingly leader.

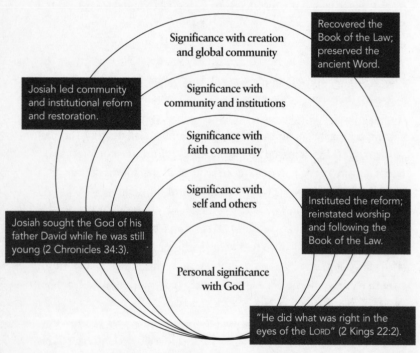

Figure 3.3. Josiah's Sphere of Significance

The Way of the Prophets

The Hebrew word for prophet, *nabî'*, carries the meaning of one who speaks for the divine. Biblically, we find two classes of prophets: those who were recognized as prophets of God and those who were rejected as false prophets. Those who were called by God to be prophets received their callings under various circumstances but always with direct communication from God. Moses was called through the burning bush on a mountain as he was keeping his family's sheep; Isaiah had a glorious vision of God being high and lifted up; Jeremiah was known by God to be a prophet while he was in his mother's womb, and God spoke this role into his realization while he was yet young. Huldah, Micah, Amos, Habakkuk, and others were also recognized as prophets, and many of their writings are preserved for us in Scripture.

Their Service
The prophets played significant roles in their communities and in their countries: giving God's message to the people. Called to specific geographical areas, some prophets served in their home communities while others served God's people across national boundaries. Some spoke to the northern kingdom of Israel from the southern kingdom of Judah, and others sent word to the exiles in Babylon from their distant homeland of Jerusalem. In their work, they sometimes spoke truth to power and other times spoke truth to people. Theirs was not an easy task on any front. The prophets spoke justice to injustice, righteousness to unrighteousness, hope to hopelessness, repentance to rebellion, faithfulness to infidelity, peace to strife, belonging to the lost, God's love to the loveless, and punishment to the disobedient, making their messages of two natures, hope or doom. The hope involved the promised Messiah, the remnant that would return from exile, and the expectation of a liberated kingdom.

About the call and work of the prophets, we have 2 Peter 1:19-21:

> We also have the prophetic message as something completely reliable, and you will do well to pay attention to it, as to a light shining in a dark place, until the day dawns and the morning star rises in your hearts. Above all, you must understand that no prophecy of Scripture came about by the prophet's own interpretation of things. For prophecy never had its origin in the human will, but prophets, though human, spoke from God as they were carried along by the Holy Spirit.

Their Spiritual Practices

Joan Chittister, a Benedictine sister and theologian, describes the biblical prophets in ways that help us see that they were real human beings who were no different than we are. Chittister says, "all of them were simple souls like you and me. All of them loved without limit, burned with an enduring patience, were afire with God, and proclaimed a new vision. All of them invite you and me to claim our prophetic dimension and speak God's work in the midst of human chaos." For Chittister prophecy is not a peripheral; it is an essential dimension of the religious life.[4]

These "simple souls" were sustained in their work by a faithful adherence to spiritual practices or disciplines that were probably motivated more by their desire for relationship with the Divine than by any prescribed way of being. Patterns of practice that were rooted in their religious identity, worship and service to the Lord Yahweh, and later biblical Judaism can be observed. Those practices are covered under the traditional categories as listed below.

Internal	External
Prayer	Offerings
Fasting	Service
Meditation	Observing Sabbath
Solitude	

Supported by such a set of practices, the prophets were inspired to listen and perceive as God interacted with them. They were responsible for discerning God's direction and intent to resolve the circumstances and situations of their day—relational situations between Yahweh and Israel, between Israel and others, between people and power, between God and their systems.

We find this to be so through the prophetic work of Micah: "What does the LORD require of you? To act justly and to love mercy and to walk humbly with your God" (Micah 6:8). We hear it through God's message delivered to the people through Jeremiah: "For I know the plans I have for you," declares the LORD, "plans to prosper you and not to harm you, plans to give you hope and a future" (Jeremiah 29:11). And Isaiah delivered messages of both doom and hope: because of sin, God would punish Israel, yet because of God's love and grace, they would be restored when they repented.

> Woe to those who make unjust laws,
> to those who issue oppressive decrees,
> to deprive the poor of their rights
> and withhold justice from the oppressed of my people,
> making widows their prey
> and robbing the fatherless.
> What will you do on the day of reckoning,
> when disaster comes from afar?
> To whom will you run for help?
> Where will you leave your riches?
> Nothing will remain but to cringe among the captives
> or fall among the slain.
> Yet for all this, his anger is not turned away,
> his hand is still upraised.
>
> —Isaiah 10:1-5

Ezekiel opened one of his passages by saying, "The word of the LORD came to me" (Ezekiel 33:1). God was calling him to be a watchman. God said to Ezekiel, "So you, mortal, I have made a sentinel for the house of Israel; whenever you hear a word from my mouth, you shall give them warning from me" (33:7, NRSV).

There are very good resources on prophetic spirituality and the manner in which prophetic work can be observed and performed today. Jan Garrett, writer of an essay titled "Prophetic Spirituality," says that prophetic spirituality is "a way of being religious imbued with a burning concern for social justice and the improvement of flawed social institutions."5

Many of us have this prophetic spirituality as part of our charism, or spiritual power. This spirituality accompanies the piety that is generally understood as our inward or internal spiritual disciplines. When we look at the historic prophets, we see that they held fast to their piety while also living out their assigned prophetic work. But our piety alone can leave us, as what I often heard growing up in my church, so "heavenly minded that we are of no earthly good." Being of "earthly good" involved serving God and others along with maintaining a pious life.

We were taught that pious living is aimed at walking in a way that pleases God. It is part of our formation, our discipleship. And in this prophetic tradition, we were trained to be involved in issues of justice, peace, and equality so that we might bring God's will into our reality and into that of our neighbors near or far.

One who knew the need for prophetic work, Ann Frank, a Jewish victim of the Holocaust, wrote, "I know what I want, I have a goal, an opinion, I have a religion and love. Let me be myself and then I am satisfied. I know that I'm a woman, a woman with inward strength and plenty of courage. If God lets me live . . . I shall not remain insignificant, I shall work in the world and for mankind! And now I know that first and foremost I shall require courage and cheerfulness."6 We know that Ann Frank died in 1945 just before her liberation. But her significance comes through the writings she left in her diary, which captured her observations of the experience in hiding and in Auschwitz. Her voice still speaks through those pages and has played a significant role in teaching the world of the effects of discrimination and persecution.

This prophetic *way*, of course, culminates in the life and model of Jesus and will be discussed later in this chapter.

The Historical Period

What we designate as the historical period in the Hebrew Scriptures might also be designated the era of Exile and Restoration. It encompasses the centuries after Israel (the Northern Kingdom) and Judah (the Southern Kingdom) have been carried into captivity by Assyria and Babylon, respectively, when God's people are struggling to understand what it means to be God's people when the Promised Land and the holy city of Jerusalem have been lost to pagan foreign invaders. It was during this era that many of the prophets spoke, proclaiming words of both judgment and encouragement to the people who survived and struggled to keep their faith alive.

Esther
Esther is one who lived her call to radical faith and service during that painful and tenuous time of the Old Testament. A young Jewish woman, she was selected as queen by the Persian king Xerxes after he disposed of Queen Vashti for her resistance to his demeaning demands and expectations. Esther kept her cultural, ethnic, and religious identity hidden from the king as she had been told to do by her cousin Mordecai (Esther 2:7). She found favor with the king above all other young women, so he crowned her queen.

Positioned in a High Place
This popular biblical story is about this beautiful young woman who is challenged to see that her positioning within the king's house is not for her glory but for her to bring glory to God. Her charge is not to keep

safe but to keep faithful—faithful to God, faithful to herself, and faithful to her people. Again we see God calling someone to be the right person in the right place at the right time and for the right purpose.

Purposed in a High Place

Esther was strategically positioned in such a high place, the king's house, for a purpose. People are strategically positioned to be used by God every day. Esther's people were going to be destroyed. Who she really was would be revealed in God's purpose. Would she be safe? Her uncle said, "Do not think that because you are in the king's house you alone of all the Jews will escape. For if you remain silent at this time, relief and deliverance for the Jews will arise from another place, but you and your father's family will perish. And who knows but that you have come to your royal position for such a time as this?" (Esther 4:13-14).

Prayerful in a High Place

In her response, Esther gave a faithful witness to her faith and spiritual practice. She requested that all the Jews fast night and day for three days for her. Forbidden to go before the king without first being summoned to come, the penalty of which was death, she would risk her life to deliver a request for her people to be spared. An answer to the call of God like this cannot be done without fasting and prayer. She vowed to go to the king after three days, saying those profound words, "And if I perish, I perish" (Esther 4:16).

Protected in a High Place

Positioned, purposed, prayerful, and protected, Esther did not perish. Perhaps it was the condition of her heart, the willingness of her spirit, the strength of her faith, the depth of her love, or the sensing of her season that moved Esther to act. As a result, her people were protected and Esther as well, to the glory of God. The witness of Esther compels us to consider our own significance and the way God places us to use us for God's purpose—sometimes in high places.

The Way of Jesus

Jesus, through life application, leads humanity on the path to salvation and also on the road of righteousness and justice. This is the work of discipleship. This is the work of the church, the body of Christ, present and active in the realities of our time. We are sustained by our faithful devotion to having a relationship with our loving God. God desires not only to be in relationship with us but also to inspire us and direct our activity that we might live significant lives full of meaning and purpose.

His Identity
It is not until you have touched your finger to the flame that you can know the real meaning of the candle. To say that Jesus lived a significant life on earth is a flagrant understatement. Jesus—born in humble surroundings, the son of a teen mother, raised by a skilled laborer, yet Son of God. He came full of the Spirit and in the image of God not only to point humanity to right relationship with God but also to direct humanity toward right relationship with humanity. Jesus' mission statement, found in Luke 4:18, is a plan to do just that. It reads: "The Spirit of the Lord is upon me, because he has anointed me to bring good news to the poor. He has sent me to proclaim release to the captives and recovery of sight to the blind, to let the oppressed go free" (NRSV).

His Work and Model
Jesus' mission plan's primary subjects are the poor, the brokenhearted, prisoners, the blind, and the oppressed. His is redemptive, prophetic, liberating, and relational work. He does this through preaching, healing, giving, liberating, proclaiming, dying, and rising. He provided a model of this work of God for centuries to come and for today. Authentic prophetic ministry follows Jesus' model—Jesus' way.

Throughout the Gospels the record of Jesus' work is presented in the accounts of eyewitnesses who saw what Jesus did, heard what he said, and witnessed the results. In his life and ministry, Jesus demonstrated and taught his disciples how a prophetic ministry would bring in the kingdom of God. The church is the body of Christ living prophetically in our homes, our neighborhoods, our workplaces, our cities and towns, our country, and our world.

When we follow Jesus' ministry model; when we live Spirit-filled lives, having touched our finger to the flame; when we see that Jesus' way of loving, of being, of serving is real, that indeed his way is both powerful and purposeful, then we can know about the candle. We can only touch our finger to the flame—to the essence of Jesus—when we get activated as Jesus did. We have to move from the garden to the gates, from the boat to the borders, from the pews to the people. Below is a look at what could be at the least a partial sphere of significance for Jesus—partial, because no diagram can fully and comprehensively capture the scope of Jesus Christ.

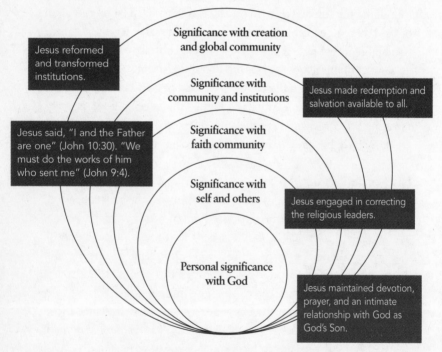

Figure 3.4. Jesus' Partial Sphere of Significance

The Way of the Early Church

The New Testament church is a formation that we can observe through the historical and testimonial record of the Scriptures, specifically from the book of Acts through the Epistles. The early church is launched in Acts 2 with the account of the day of Pentecost, when the Holy Spirit descends, empowering and anointing many who are present, including the disciples. From there the early church begins to address the questions of meaning and purpose that arise from this new track of faith. Those who claim belief in Jesus are following the leadership of the apostles, learning what their own religious practice will mean for them, their families, and communities as Jews and as Gentiles. In general they begin to respond to their personal religious experience but also to their public contextual challenges.

Responding to Contextual Challenges

As the early church was forming and growing, they had issues and challenges as would be expected given the culture: a mix of Roman, Greek, and Jewish believers; varying religious traditions among Jews, both Grecian and Hebraic; the politics of the Roman government; socioeconomic diversity; changing roles for women in society and in religion; and issues of vulnerable children and widows. Economic challenges surfaced in financing this new faith community. Luke 20:25 is an example of how Jesus responded to questions about citizenship and paying taxes. Paul, whom we know was a Roman citizen, continued Jesus' instruction in Romans 13, where he exhorts believers to give allegiance to the earthly rulers, making for good citizenship, while simultaneously focusing on their faithful citizenship in God's kingdom.

One of the early church's greatest challenges was participating in the earthly world while being citizens of the heavenly kingdom. Paul wrote in his letter to the Romans that we believers should not be conformed to the standards of this world but be transformed by the renewing of our minds (12:2). He went even further, telling the church how to be countercultural in chapter 12, verses 9 through 21, concluding with "Do not be overcome by evil, but overcome evil with good." Paul was thrown into prison, accused of treason against the government for promoting a new king in Jesus Christ. He was ordered to cease preaching the gospel. Paul's response was allegiance to his calling and vocation. He preached and advanced the gospel to the guards and other prisoners, convicting and converting them.

The issue of Jews associating with Gentiles was a contextual reality addressed by both Peter and Paul. Peter's clearest example was his visit to Cornelius's house in Caesarea. The Gentile Cornelius, having all his family and friends there at his house, set up a challenging dynamic for Peter, for he had formerly been taught not to associate with Gentiles. He said to them, "You are well aware that it is against our law for a Jew to associate with or visit a Gentile. But God has shown me that I should not call anyone impure or unclean. So when I was sent for, I came without raising any objection" (Acts 10:28). Peter was taught this through a vision of unclean animals in a sheet while he was hungry. Seeing only the unclean animals in the vision, which according to Jewish law were not to be eaten, a voice told Peter to eat because God has made clean what was once called impure (Acts 10:9-16). Jesus taught Peter (and other Christians to come) that he has come for everyone, not just for some. Those at Cornelius's house received the Holy Spirit and were baptized in the name of Jesus Christ.

Beginning with the stoning of Stephen, the early church was moved out from its center in Jerusalem to the other surrounding regions, cities, and towns. What began in fear and a desperate pursuit of survival soon became the strongest witness of the believers. From Jerusalem they scattered into locations that held more challenges that would be addressed by Jesus' disciples and apostles. Scripture preserves a record of such responses through the Epistles, especially Paul's letters to the churches.

How did they go about making decisions as they encountered these challenges? Consideration had to be given to diversity, leadership struggles, transitional challenges, care of the community, and matters of holiness while living among pagans and nonbelievers.

Care of the Church Community

One specific challenge in the early church was the equal distribution of food among the widows of the new Christian community. While the apostles were preaching and teaching, a dispute was going on over the fairness of treatment of the local widows in the Jerusalem community and those who were deemed outsiders because of their identification with the Greek culture. This problem was resolved by the apostles asking the congregation of disciples to select from among themselves people who could "wait on tables" (Acts 6:2). This was an inclusive and participative community decision made not by the apostles but by the community. They chose seven individuals who were reputable, wise, and full of the Holy Spirit.

This action resolved that particular contextual matter of diversity and fairness (Acts 6:1-7). Ensuring that there would be no differentiation made between culturally diverse groups in this newly forming community of believers in Christ was an important first act. How it was handled demonstrates the importance of equity, inclusion, participation, and community involvement in decision making where appropriate.

In any context, some kind of diversity will challenge leaders in their efforts to assist with meeting the needs of the community. On other occasions, we read that the apostles (most often Peter or Paul) made the decisions as the leadership of the church. They did so with the mind of Christ and the leading of the Holy Spirit (Acts 10).

Financing the Church and Mission

Addressing the question of financing this new church and its mission was an early challenge for the apostles. In Acts 3 we see the forming community coming together in *koinonia*, or fellowship. In *koinonia* all things are shared and thus held in common. This was as much economic as it was relational. There was enough for all. This is contrasted with the action of Ananias and Sapphira (Acts 5:1-11), whose example demonstrated that holding back, holding out, and deceit are not acceptable.

This new spiritual mission would be driven by the believers' belief in the gospel and commitment to walking as witnesses. They would be shaped and developed for their spiritual work through the presence of the Holy Spirit and God's provision of spiritual gifts. In Paul's letter to the Roman church, he explains how God distributes those gifts (see Romans 12).

Motivating Mission through Spiritual Gifts

Spiritual gifts—supernatural, God-given abilities, qualities, or aware-ness—were activated by the Holy Spirit in the early church. God pro-vides an inner urge to energize our drive toward the work that God has for us to do. This inner urge, as I call it, is the "if your gift is . . ." in Romans 12:6-8. By substituting the word *urge*, as in a compelling drive, for the word *gift*, we get the sense of the motivating nature of these gifts. The spiritual gifts are accompanied by a diversity of urges or strong nudges. "If you have a strong urge to prophesy, then prophesy. If you have a compelling urge to serve, then serve," and so on.

Addressing the diversity of work, Paul began with the diversity of gifts, as found in 1 Corinthians 12. These gifts are not given for person-al gain but rather, as stated in verse 7, "for the common good"—the good of the community. The mission is further supported through the offices of the church described in Ephesians 4:11, offices that are estab-lished to equip the people for the works of service so that the body of Christ may be built up. These offices include apostles, prophets, evan-gelists, pastors, and teachers.

With all of these gifts and offices, believers are prepared to embark on a sustained life of ministry and mission that is initiated, instituted, and incorporated into the full work of Christ in the world. This mission will continue until Christ comes again.

People of "The Way"

The New Testament references believers as "people of the Way" (see Acts 9:2; 19:9; 19:23; 22:4; 24:14). This wording first shows up in Acts 9, when Saul of Tarsus (before his conversion to the apostle Paul) uses this label when asking the high priest for letters to imprison any men or women he may find who belong to the Way. Jesus had said of himself that he is "the way and the truth and the life" (John 14:6). Thus, the Way is Jesus, the living God; and people of the Way are his followers. At Antioch Jesus' followers were first called Christians (Acts 11:26).

The early people of the Way followed Jesus in their lifestyle, their witness, and their work; and the mission and model of the early church became a pattern to be followed and further developed as the witness of the church moved on across time and culture.

Notes

1. Myoung Suk Ja is a Zen monk who is referred to by Barbara Ellen Bowe in *Biblical Foundations of Spirituality: Touching a Finger to the Flame* (Lanham, MD: Rowman & Littlefield, 2003), 2.

2. Barbara E. Bowe, *Biblical Foundations of Spirituality*, 4.

3. The emphasis in the quote is in the original text. Charles H. Spurgeon, "Effectual Calling—Illustrated by the Call of Abram," in Metropolitan Tabernacle Pulpit, Vol. 14, 1868. Sermon 843, www.spurgeongems.org.

4. This is a quote from an interview with Joan Chittister for an E-Course on Spirituality and Practuce online, "The Cry of the Prophet: An Online Retreat and Practice Group." www.spiritualityandpractice.com/prophet.

5. Jan Garrett, "Prophetic Spirituality", July 1998, www.people.wku.edu/jan.garrett/prophet.htm.

6. Ann Frank, "If God Lets Me Live I Shall Attain," *Dictionary.com*, http:quotes.dictionary.com/If_God_Lets_Me_Live_I_Shall_Attain.

CHAPTER 4

Spirituality across Time and Cultures

Our deepest calling is to grow into our own authentic self-hood, whether or not it conforms to some image of who we ought to be. As we do so, we will not only find the joy that every human being seeks—we will also find our path of authentic service in the world.

—Parker J. Palmer [1]

Varying spiritual practices rest within the stream of Christian spiritual traditions that have emerged and evolved down through the ages. These traditions have been formed across cultures, contexts, nations, and ethnicities, and among diverse Christian church bodies and movements. By necessity this chapter will provide a very cursory overview of the evolution of such traditions and practices, but it will serve our purposes in providing the connection of the spirituality we experience that is engaged and active in our surroundings and circumstances of the day.

These traditions form a stream or streams that have not just influenced institutions, religion, and practice over time, but that have also been formative in shaping how we have come to know ourselves. These "legacies," as I will call them here, have been carried on in the stories of their direct descendants. Parker Palmer understands this as authentic selfhood, as expressed in the epigraph above. For centuries Christian spirituality has been emerging and evolving toward a more deeply lived, expansive, and relevant way within changing cultures, contexts, and communities.

Church Fathers and Mothers

In his book *Historical Christianity: African Centered*, author James C. Anyike discusses the church fathers as African men who are celebrated forerunners in the church who marked the tradition with monasticism. Known also as the "desert fathers," such persons included Origen, the third-century church father of Alexandria; Cyprian, who was bishop of Carthage; and Augustine of Hippo, who is known for saying of our desire for God, "You have made us for yourself, and our hearts are restless until they find their rest in you."[2] The desert fathers had a significant influence over the development of the early Christian church.[3]

Christian monasticism was a life set apart to be in the religious community but also to minister in the wider community. If we accept that African Christians developed various forms of synthesis between Christianity and local religions, then it follows that an African-centered spirituality in the Christian tradition would incorporate in it African values, perceptions, beliefs, and practices. Among those spiritual values is the value of community over the individual and the priority of the common good, sharing what one has for the good of the community. This is consistent with Acts 2.

Roman Catholic Practices

There are an enormous number of charisms[4] within Roman Catholicism. Yet some of them stand out as mainline Catholic spiritualities, such as Jesuit (Spanish and Italian), Franciscan (Italian), and Carmelite (Spanish and French). I had firsthand experience with learning and observing Franciscan spirituality while employed at a university sponsored by the Order of the Sisters of Saint Francis of Assisi (OSF) in Milwaukee, Wisconsin. Francis of Assisi is one of the most popular (and often quoted) saints known to Catholics and non-Catholics alike. Among the most popular of the sayings attributed to Francis is "Preach the gospel always, and when necessary use words."

Clare of Assisi (1194–1253) was among the first followers of Francis and his way of life. She was eighteen years old when she heard Francis preaching and was called to more deeply follow Christ and vowed to give herself to a life of service. Clare could not join in with Francis and his brothers because she was a woman, but she continued learning and following God's will in her life with Francis's guidance and leadership. Clare's example attracted other women, and with the blessing of Francis, they cofounded a new order, the Order of Poor Ladies, also known as the Poor Clares. Francis and Clare left their wealth, privilege, and families to accept calls to live out the gospel serving the poor, the oppressed, and the afflicted.[5]

Richard Rohr, author and Franciscan priest of the New Mexico Province and the founder of the Center for Action and Contemplation, in his book *Eager to Love: The Alternative Way of Francis of Assisi*, says of them both,

> Francis and Clare were not so much prophets by what they said as in the radical, system-critiquing way that they lived their lives. They found both their inner and outer freedom by structurally living on the edge of the inside of both church and society . . . Francis and Clare's agenda for justice was the most fundamental and under-cutting of all others: a very simple lifestyle outside the system of production and consumption (the real meaning of the vow of poverty), plus a conscious identification with the marginalized of society (the communion of saints pushed to its outer edge).[6]

Keith Douglass Warner, in a paper on Franciscan spirituality, provides a very clear and concise distinction of the Franciscan *spiritual* tradition as compared with other traditions. He says that the difference is not monastic, because Franciscan spirituality promotes public preaching and social engagement. It is not strictly apostolic, because it is also grounded in the practice of community living and contemplative prayer. So Franciscan living is to live the gospel as a framework for life—*evangelical life*.[7]

The Franciscan Federation, in their 2008 booklet *Guidelines for the Development of the Franciscan Person*, identifies a model for a Franciscan. Among these spiritual characteristics are the following:

Conversion. Conversion is characteristic of Franciscan spirituality, which indicates turning to God and being conformed to Christ. In this order, conversion is considered to be an ongoing, lifelong process of becoming. Francis converted from a self-focus to Other/others focus in which he left the privileged life he had and took on the life of the poor and the marginalized. This was an ongoing process for Francis. Clare was converted in/by a role of leadership through a changed understanding. In *Guidelines for the Development of the Franciscan Person*, conversion is explained as a "movement, not a moment. It is a constant giving of self over to the Spirit. One's vision of life is renewed. Conversion continually clarifies and fine-tunes the vision."[8]

Contemplation. Another characteristic of Franciscan spirituality is praying both privately and together so that the participants' hearts are free to consult and seek the advice of others in discerning God's will. An emphasis here is that the "foundation of the spiritual life is intimacy with the Spirit of the Lord."[9]

Minoritas and poverty. The word *minoritas* used by Francis means "minority and/or humility." Having an attitude of *minoritas* and poverty, which means not clinging to power, privilege, or prestige but having the posture of a servant and humility, is characterstic of Franciscans.[10] From my pilgrimage learning (I have made two pilgrimages to Assisi), I understood this to mean that to be a minority, or *minor*, is to be humble. It is to think of yourself as lower than others in power and privilege. I accept and seek to exemplify humility in my life as Christ-like but I must admit that, personally, I found the language of this particular Franciscan characteristic to be difficult to connect with as a position of choice coming from the historical standpoint of myself as an African American, given the African Americans' struggles in America. In this personal social sense, after having been relegated to a *minority* status not just demographically but socially and politically as well through oppression, human degradation, and disempowerment, choosing to take a position of minor, poverty, and lower than others in power and privilege was a concept that I found myself wrestling with. Yet, I do strive to live with Christ-like humility and perhaps that, in the end, is the overall goal of this Franciscan characteristic.

Fraternal life. This characteristic is the understanding that to live as sisters and brothers in Christ is to live in full communion, in community, in mutual relationship. *Guidelines for the Development of the Franciscan Person* points to the Trinity as the model of this dynamic relationship, the persons gifting one another with life-giving love and goodness.[11] This communal life is more than being interdependent; it is living in full mutuality. I connect this dynamic to the pattern of life we read about in the latter part of Acts 2, the fellowship of the believers.

Peacemaking. Characteristic of Franciscan spirituality is to be an instrument of peace. I have experienced peacemaking efforts of Franciscans, both employees and students, during my employment at Cardinal Stritch University in Milwaukee, a Franciscan institution. All were encouraged to be peacemakers in personal relationships and in the larger community. Peacemaking in society could include writing letters to legislators to end war, volunteering at a homeless shelter to show compassion and care, or seeking reconciliation where there were disputes.

Mission. Revealing God, God's love, and the reign of God by serving among the poor, "preaching" the gospel, and practicing mutuality in giving and in receiving are at the heart of the Franciscan identity as they seek to live as Jesus lived to show God's love to the world.

Church. A final characteristic of Franciscan spirituality is remaining in relationship with the Roman Catholic Church as Francis and Clare did during their lives in the church of their times.[12]

This model of the Franciscan life provides a concise understanding of Franciscan spirituality that has been followed not only by Catholics but by non-Catholics as well.

Eastern Orthodox Tradition

When it comes to their position on social justice and spirituality, the Eastern Orthodox Church focuses on one-on-one direct relationships and true love of neighbor. In response to needs in the world, Orthodox Christians show love by serving their needy neighbors. Educator Ann Bezzerides discusses how the tradition of the Orthodox Church regarding social justice is to oppose political and power structures by working to empower individuals. She says that empowerment is inconsistent with the Orthodox spirituality of living in the posture of humility.[13] This "inconsistency" relating to empowerment, I think, is akin to what was stated earlier about Franciscan spirituality in which to be humble is to think of yourself as lower in power and privilege than others. As such, for the Orthodox, needy neighbors are served with good deeds, provision, and aid but they are not taught to be empowered. Bezzerides more deeply discusses current considerations being given to the question of how to teach Orthodox youth the traditions of the Orthodox church and reflect upon the thought and practices regarding social justice. The term social justice, according to Bezzerides, should be omitted from use as it is popularly understood. Social justice is considered divisive and to have a political agenda.[14]

Without delving further into the very complex matter of Orthodoxy, something I have little direct knowledge of, I take away from Bezzerides's article that historically the Orthodox Church has not maintained a highly public voice on social questions. However, their spiritual mandate on love of neighbor and the sacredness of the human person created in the image of God is at the center of their social theology rather than political, philosophical, or social progress. The Orthodox Church historically has had a strong social witness, a witness that brings spiritual transformation of persons first, and then transformed persons transform society. However, there is a sense of this social witness needing a revival in such a way that it "begins with the person who, transformed by the Gospel, takes that message and that living example of Christian charity to the wider worlds. The transformation of the heart can and must lead to the transformation of society."[15] A very defining quote on this tradition comes from John Chrysostom: "I beg you, remember this without fail, that not to share our own wealth with the poor is theft from the poor and deprivation of their means of life. We do not possess our own wealth but theirs."[16] This, however, does not excuse persons from their own responsibilities and enterprise. It is the transformed heart that will both seek to live such a life and witness to that love by serving the needy neighbor.

Reformation and Revivalist Spiritualities

The Protestant Reformers of the sixteenth century, prominently led by John Calvin and Huldrych Zwingli, were responding to what they saw as a decline in personal spiritual practices among the then mainline churches. Interestingly, Calvin is quoted as saying that "a spiritual life that does not issue forth in works of love to those close and those distant, and in social justice, is not true spirituality."[17] The denominations in the United States that are usually considered to be part of the Reformed tradition include the Presbyterians, the Reformed Church of America, the Christian Reformed Church, and (though it can be debated) the Disciples of Christ. Persons in the Anabaptist, Baptist, Methodist, and Anglican traditions have also been strongly influenced by the Reformed tradition.

The revivalist movement that followed along in this period of spiritual awakening was considered as part of a continuum. The movement sought to change persons who would in turn transform society. This strongly evangelistic spirituality was about living a personal experience with God and then changing the cultural and societal experience to reflect the kingdom of God.

Social Gospel

Walter Rauschenbusch is most noted as the father of the social gospel movement. Born in 1861, Rauschenbusch began his ministry in the ghettos of the Lower East Side of New York. According to William Brackney, in his article "Baptists in Transformation: American Baptist Contributions," it was while Rauschenbusch was pastoring there that he "observed with horror and compassion the working and living conditions of immigrants in the eastern cities and concluded there was deepening social sin that prevented realization of the literal Kingdom of God."[18]

Brackney says this personal experience, combined with Rauschenbusch's understanding of the reign of God, formed Rauschenbusch's theology toward a social gospel—a theology that sees the intersection of God's desire for humanity and "ethics among Baptists." This social gospel created the movement of justice in an unjust society, an ethical and moral foundation that would bolster and spur acts of justice, known as social justice as well as spiritual and social activism.

What impact did this theological awakening have on Rauschenbusch? It did for him as God aims for us. Brackney says that, "transformed personally, Walter tackled problems of greed in the accumulation of industrial capital; he strove for imposition of working standards for women and children; and he contended for the recognition and rights of women."[19] Brackney further explains that Rauschenbush "introduced a new doctrine of humanity, a new understanding of sinfulness that amounted to structural evil in institutions, and a broader definition of salvation that included the social context, . . . "[20] This theological lens and stance opens the way for the gospel to speak to the justice issues and social conditions of his time and times to come.

We can see the "Rauschenbusch effect" in the many social justice works worldwide. The work of the social gospel movement is to be pursued even now. Any institution, system, policy, or person that demeans and destroys human integrity by any law, any institution, or any conceived notion is to be confronted and converted.

Abolitionist Movement

The trading and ownership of persons of African descent for slavery in the United States and the Caribbean during the eighteenth and nineteenth centuries was one of those ethical, moral, and theological issues that violated God's vision for the humanity of the kingdom of God. This violation of God's purposes had to be addressed as both mission and ministry. The movement to abolish slavery was an example of a social system being confronted by the might of a theological and spiritual response—a mission purpose. This was a response that was called for by belief and conviction and was spirited by the demand for righteousness and justice. Here was a church motivated to activism against government, enterprise, neighbor, and even church member.

In 1845 a Baptist mission-sending denominational organization struck a strong position of not commissioning anyone to missionary service who held slaves. This decision resulted in splitting the North American Baptists between Northern and Southern churches. And the continuation of this progressive stance resulted in the sending of African Americans to missionary work overseas—including Lulu Fleming, the first African American female missionary, to the Congo in 1887; Lott Carey to Africa; and George Leile to the Caribbean Islands. It also resulted in supporting missionaries to work in the southern United States with freed men, women, and children; and in establishing schools that exist to this day to educate young African American women and men, such as Shaw University and Spelman and Morehouse Colleges.

Baptists were not the only church body to respond to antislavery. William Wilberforce, John Wesley, and the Quakers were all active in abolition in England.

Quakers
Even those who claim to be authorities on Quaker history and practice acknowledge the challenge they have in giving a specific definition of this unique religious tradition. What can be said is that Quaker spiritu-

ality has a lot in common with the spirituality and work that have been present in a social witness through activism and social transformation. Quakers lean strongly on the workings of the inward life—that is, living with a deep sense of relationship with God, practicing a holy listening for the presence of God speaking and guiding, and having their own sense of that inner voice. In his book *Let Your Life Speak: Listening for the Voice of Vocation*, Parker J. Palmer explains the voice of vocation this way: "Before you tell your life what you will do with it, listen for what your life wants to do with you."[21] The point that Palmer makes is that our vocation, a word that comes from the Latin *vocaré*, meaning "to voice or to call," comes from within us. It is work of the interior that leads to the outward work.

Social justice and social activism are inherent in Quaker piety. Historically we can point to the work of the Quakers in the abolitionist movement. It is a matter of conscience and conviction that oppression should not be inflicted on any person who shares in the same "inner light" as another who bears that light. Beginning with their own leaders, Quaker abolitionists worked to bring about systemic and social change, not as a purely social matter but also as a spiritual one.

Baptists

I took a seminary course in Baptist spirituality in 1996 while in my doctoral program. The professor opened the course by observing that most people don't recognize Baptists as having an identifiable Baptist spirituality. Of course, this was both surprising and off-putting to the Baptists in the room. His point was that Baptists are of such diverse identities and traditions that pinning down a prescribed spirituality is a challenge.

The professor did, however, go on to identify some distinguishing marks acknowledged as indicators of a spirituality that has been expressed in Baptists' activity in the world. The closest models, he observed, come from John Bunyan, a seventeenth-century English pastor most famous for writing the allegory *Pilgrim's Progress*, and Martin

Luther King Jr., the twentieth-century African American pastor and civil rights leader famous for his "I Have a Dream" speech, his nonviolent protests, and his assassination in 1968.

Drawing from these examples, Baptist spirituality can be given a description, recognizing, however, that Baptists are not monolithic. It is a longstanding joke that you can ask ten Baptists to address any given topic and get ten different responses. Therefore, it is with a measure of humility that I offer a gathered perspective that I hope will lead to further development and discussion as it relates to Baptist spirituality and social transformation.

Following are seven keys to Baptist spirituality. Baptists are

- prayerful
- Bible-centered
- service-minded
- mission-oriented
- social justice-minded
- activist-oriented
- prone to suffering for the cause of Christ

Of course, Baptists can vary in their specific and particular sense of engagement, activism, and related theology. There are diverse Baptist denominations with particularities that distinguish how they live out their work and mission. I discuss how Baptists engage in service and mission in later chapters.

The Salvation Army

The Salvation Army was founded in 1865 in London by onetime Methodist minister William Booth, who gave up the "comfort of his pulpit and decided to take his message into the streets where it would reach the poor, the homeless, the hungry and the destitute."[22] The Salvation Army is regarded as a prime example of the servant church model. "'Saved to serve,' or 'Serve to save,'" is what two of my Salvationist friends said in unison when I spoke with them about the mission of the Salvation Army.

Booth started out to evangelize those who were poor to bring them into the church. "Thieves, prostitutes, gamblers, and [alcoholics] were among Booth's first converts to Christianity." He soon found out that the poor, homeless, and destitute did not feel any more comfortable in these churches as did the church members feel comfortable having such people with them.[23] So William Booth began a church especially for those who were being reached.

Today the Salvation Army is an international movement with missions and churches all over the world, including the United States. The Army's mission is "to preach the gospel of Jesus Christ and to meet human needs in his name without discrimination."[24] The work of the Salvation Army is very evident in most U.S. communities. They operate resale stores that make clothing, appliances, furniture, and a wide variety of other items available to people who otherwise would not be able to afford the things they need. When disaster strikes—such as a tornado or a family being burned out of their home—the Army responds by providing shelter, food, and clothing.

"One Army, one mission, one message" is the Salvation Army's vision tag line. Elements of their vision include the following:

One Mission. Into the world of the hurting, broken, lonely, dispossessed and lost, reaching them in love by all means, we will

■ emphasize our integrated ministry
■ reach and involve youth and children
■ stand for and serve the marginalized
■ encourage innovation in mission

One Message. With the transforming message of Jesus, bringing freedom, hope and life, we will

- communicate Christ unashamedly
- reaffirm our belief in transformation
- evangelize and disciple effectively
- provide quality teaching resources[25]

The Army's vision is carried out today through the provision of community support ministries, such as adult rehabilitation, veterans' affairs services, prison ministries, services for the elderly, programs to combat human trafficking, youth camps and recreation, hunger relief, and housing and homeless services. Probably most associated with the Salvation Army are the red kettles and bell ringers who give the general public an opportunity to share in the work of the Army through money deposited in the kettles.

The Salvation Army supports the spiritual development of its members through the Center for Spiritual Life Development, which encourages following spiritual disciplines, maintaining boundless prayer, and participating in regular study. The Army currently is in a special season of reflection. A statement about this season says:

> The Salvation Army is in a time of spiritual renewal, of re-awakening to the Fire of God on the inside of people that fuels all the outward activity and service. Surely the Spirit of God is inviting The Salvation Army in these days to hear afresh the call to become a house of prayer for all nations, the place where God promised to dwell; the place where God makes himself at home.
>
> The apostle Paul admonishes, "Since we live by the Spirit, let us keep in step with the Spirit" (Galatians 5:25).
>
> We can't do God's part; he won't do ours. Hear his invitation to participate, do your part in being a center for spiritual life development.[26]

Heart to God, hand to man, saved to serve—the Salvation Army is clear about their calling.

Methodism

"We Act in Society" is the opening headline on the United Methodist Church's (UMC) Church and Society webpage. The UMC has a long history in matters of piety and social justice. This history and stance is rooted in the model of their founder, John Wesley, whose vision was reforming and transforming society through personal piety and social justice, combining faith and action. Hence the headline "We Act in Society." Wesley led the Methodists in influencing society in social justice, effecting prison reform and participating in the abolitionist movement. In the United States, Methodists were supportive of opportunities for women and of the social gospel movement.

According to David Werner, a United Methodist pastor, John Wesley asked often, "How is Your doing?" By this Wesley meant to challenge people to share how they were doing in living out their faith in action, believing it would drive them further in living changed lives. Werner states, "Indeed for Wesley, *how* one was doing internally (in one's soul) was directly connected to *what* one did, or how one lived out the Christian life externally (in one's actions)."[27] Doing comes from the soul, the heart, and the spirit, and it affects the state of the soul.

Methodism is preserved not only in the mainline United Methodist Church but also in the historically black traditions of the African Methodist Episcopal Church, African Methodist Episcopal Zion Church, and Christian Methodist Episcopal Church as a liberating act of protest against dominance and control within the wider Methodist church:

C. Eric Lincoln and Lawrence H. Mamiya, professors and authors, share a quote by John H. Satterwhite, Methodist churchman and author, that gives a reason for the emergence and existence of the black church:

> "'African' and 'Christian' in the names of our denominations denote that we are always concerned for the well-being of economically and politically exploited persons, for gaining or regaining a sense of our own future. We

must never invest with institutions that perpetrate racism. Our churches work for the change of all processes which prevent our members who are victims of racism from participating fully in civic and governmental structures.[28]

These forms of black religious independence increased the focus on race within religious expression and were expanded by the founding of the black Pentecostal churches, primarily the Church of God in Christ, but also the Holiness and Apostolic traditions. This ability to maintain independence, spiritual authenticity, self-determination, and cultural identity increased the ability of the black church to focus on and attend to the social, economic, and political conditions of African Americans. That identity and awareness became incorporated in the black church movement and in African American Christian spirituality as a whole.

The Black Church Movement

Historically speaking, many African Americans did not remain a part of the white majority denominations. The black church movement gave rise to the many black churches and denominations we have today. The black church, while not monolithic, actively kept piety, the social gospel, and the liberating message at the center of its religious and spiritual practice. The roots of African American Christian spiritual practice flow from this heritage.

Spirituality in the Black Church

When we examine African American spirituality, we do not follow the pattern of key individuals as with many of the Roman Catholic spiritualities (Francis, Ignatius, and Benedict, for example). Instead, we find a pattern of key experiences that are unique to the culture or group. These key experiences correlate with the biblical experiences of Israel's bondage and captivity and of liberation and freedom.

An examination of spirituality in the black church leads to the observation that nonwestern and even other-than-Christian spiritual traditions have been infused into the black church religious milieu. Theophus H. Smith states in his essay "The Spirituality of Afro-American Traditions" that "[African American] spirituality has achieved interreligious fusion in ways that provide an instructive model. In this model the theological expression of a people's spirituality 'has legitimated a return to the religious genius of the ancestors who came from places other than Europe.'"[29] What Smith says is instructive, as it helps to deepen an understanding of the breadth of spirituality that is operative not only within the black church but within the African American community as well. An event as simple as a family reunion can have the presence of broad religious and spiritual diversity.

Smith further cites Gayraud Wilmore, who declares the significance of black theological discourse as a model of bicultural spirituality:

> Black Theology authenticated an apprehension of Jesus of Nazareth in cultural symbols and contexts other than those of white American society. In so doing, it provides an example or model for the indigenization of theology in other societies and cultures. Subsequent developments in the United States with Hispanic, Native American, and Asian American theologies show that this de-Americanization, de-westernization of Christ opened the way for other ethnic groups to identify with him in the depths of their own historical experience.[30]

Wilmore is saying that what was experienced in the early 1980s as Afrocentricity, both theology and social thought, became prevalent within the black church. Theologians, pastors, and church members discussed Jesus' skin color, the texture of his hair, the significance of his growing years having been in Egypt, and how African traditions, principles, and spiritualities can be found in the Bible. Ethnic and cultural awareness of African American Christian spiritual identity is an increasingly popular topic of learning.

Smith says, "This growing multiethnic awareness has its parallel in Protestant churches and in Christian educational communities. The real achievements in ecumenism have also advanced interethnic awareness among various church bodies and Christian educational communities." He adds, "Beyond the national culture, however, arises the engaging opportunity for non-Western communities, particularly [developing cultures], to observe in Black experience a model for their own religious and sociopolitical transformations."[31]

Understanding that there are these levels of diversity in the black church is important. At the core of these traditions are values and principles that call for love of God and a life of prayer, engagement in and care of community, strong family ties, and service to neighbors near and far.

The experience of Christian spirituality in the African American perspective consists of at least seven basic disciplines toward living the gospel of Jesus Christ under the Holy Spirit in the presence of God. These basic disciplines are rooted in six mainline denominational and Christian church traditions: Catholics, Lutherans, Baptists, Methodists, Presbyterians, and black Pentecostals. These disciplines include the following:

■ Bible study and the regular reading of Scripture as a meditative resource
■ Other devotional writings as a source for reflection
■ Observance of the Sabbath as a day for worship, but also as a day for retreat with the engagement in creative and re-creative activity
■ Practice of daily private prayer
■ Practice of obedience to God even unto persecution
■ Participation in corporate worship
■ Active involvement in social concerns and social justice[32]

The Black Consciousness Movement

The black consciousness movement that came about in the 1960s appears to have been a revival of the rebellion and protest expressions of the earlier black evangelicalism. The precursors attributing to the movement and group identity, according to researchers Lincoln and Mamiya, were urbanization, the showing of African Americans as a distinct social group, the labor movement, the growth of black churches and associations, and the establishment of black-owned communications channels, such as radio stations, newspapers, and television programs. Also contributing to this impetus were the wars and political independence movements in Africa and the developments following the 1954 Supreme Court decision outlawing school segregation.[33]

Modern Civil Rights Era Activism

The most potent catalyst to social change brought by black church leaders was the civil rights movement led by Martin Luther King Jr., Ralph D. Abernathy, Dorothy Cotton, Fannie Lou Hamer, Ella Baker, Dorothy Height, and others. Beginning with the Montgomery bus boycott in 1955, which was triggered by Rosa Parks's refusal to conform to the demands of segregated seating on a public bus, this movement was anchored in the black church with strong leadership, financial support, and black church cultural influence.

The civil rights movement was born out of this spiritual expression of activism and the practices of prophetic preaching and of a liberating and social gospel, regular meeting for worship and prayer, valuing of community, and maintaining of regular Bible study. The black church largely provided the place, the leadership, the spiritual discipline, and the funding for the movement's efforts.[34] The characteristics listed here are at the foundation of the spiritual and social activism lived out through the civil rights movement. The movement was largely of spiritual activism at its best. The theology, moral ethics, and pursuit of a just society fueled these efforts. The leaders were predominantly ministers, joined by rabbis, priests, nuns, and sisters. This was a movement of servant leaders, everyday people, students, and church women who demonstrated prophetic and political witness.

Civil rights organizations such as the Congress of Racial Equality (CORE) and Student Nonviolent Coordinating Committee (SNCC) were launched largely by student power. C. Eric Lincoln and Lawrence H. Mamiya, in their book *The Black Church in the African American Experience*, reference Aldon Morris, author of *The Origins of the Civil Rights Movement: Black Communities Organizing for Change*, who wrote "it was the Black Church which provided an 'ideological framework through which passive attitudes were transformed into a collective consciousness supportive of collective action.'"[35]

We cannot consider the black church as representing a monolithic approach to addressing and solving the problems of African American people. Each religious persuasion can engage in a modified or entirely different form of spirituality to incorporate God's presence in the lives of African American people.

Black Nationalism

Black nationalism was an expression of an even deeper level of consciousness that was voiced by Malcolm X and the Nation of Islam. In his book *Empower the People: Social Ethics for the African American Church,* Theodore Walker Jr. says, "We are a church people. It is essential to see that we are a religious people. God-consciousness is an essential part of our self-understanding. It is the tradition of Africans almost everywhere to conceive of ourselves always in relation to God."[36] This God-consciousness is the thread of the common religious identity of African peoples across the diaspora.

Walker goes on to say that the black church is not Protestant in the sense of having protested Catholicism, but it is "protestant" in the sense of having been born in protest against domination and oppression by white Euro-American denominations and churches. The black church revolution, therefore, was about African Americans leaving white churches and denominations to form their own. "Radical and revolutionary struggle for liberation, for justice, and for empowerment is at the very heart of our religious heritage," concludes Walker.[37]

The path of African spirituality into the American diaspora leads us to an awareness of the diversity of our spiritual expressions as a people. Yet this path also leads us to our common threads that are consistent throughout all of our expressions of spirituality.

Church Women Activism

Christian women who led missions and "women's" ministries within the church made a historic expansion of their work as early as the 1870s, involving themselves in the social justice concerns of their time. They formed women's clubs, organizations, associations, societies, and conventions. "Church women," as they have been notably called, have responded to issues relating to race, gender, women and children, education, business, and health. Women joined together in interracial organizations, across denominational lines, and within all denominations. This work was done through organizations such as the Women's Home Mission Society (1877) (American Baptist Churches USA), the Baptist Woman's Convention (1900) (National Baptist Convention of the USA), the National Council of Negro Women (1875), Church Women United (1941), National Association of Colored Women's Clubs (1896), and more.

Among the earliest of the women's mission groups was the Chicago-based Women's Baptist Home Mission Society, founded in 1877, which was formed in response to women being excluded from missionary appointments to serve in areas of the United States. Young Joanna P. Moore became the first woman to be commissioned as a missionary. Moore served in the South, teaching freed blacks to read, becoming an evangelist throughout Louisiana, creating the Fireside Schools, and founding a monthly Christian magazine called *Hope*.[38] A second society, Woman's American Baptist Home Mission Society (WABHMS), was also formed in 1877 in Boston. These two groups merged in 1909 and assumed the name Woman's American Baptist Home Mission Society. Together with the American Baptist Home Mission Society (ABHMS), these missionaries engaged in education, establishing twenty-seven institutions of higher education for freed people after the Civil War. ABHMS and WABHMS worked to secure treaties that were supportive of Native Americans and to open the Baptist Missionary Training School in Chicago, just to name two accomplishments. In 1955 the two societies merged their work.[39]

The Baptist Woman's Convention in the National Baptist Convention was formed in 1900 during the time of the women's suffrage movement. Establishing a women's convention was "hotly contested in the National Baptist Convention."[40] This organization is now known as the Woman's Auxiliary to the National Baptist Convention, USA, Inc. Their mission today is to "embrace the spirit, mind, teachings and principles of Christ in their endeavor to promote Christian education, minister to needs, and promote spiritual growth for the women of their Convention and to advance the Gospel message to people, and in particular, women in the world."[41]

Women's groups were also forming outside of denominations and the local church but largely by church women. The National Association of Colored Women was one such group that was established in the 1890s. Bettye Collier-Thomas, in her book *Jesus, Jobs, and Justice: African American Women and Religion*, says "The NACW was also another manifestation of Christian women's belief that it was their responsibility to speak for and uplift less fortunate women. They believed that women, like men, were required to address the critical race issues of the times: discrimination, segregation, lynching, suffrage, colonialism, and imperialism."[42] (For an exhaustive telling of the history and activities of the interracial, interdenominational, and particular

African American women whose work was critical during this time in the twentieth century, I recommend reading this book.

Spirituality across time, culture, and traditions has emerged and evolved to be a dynamic and essential practice of faith in action. The many movements and developments have provided for the many accomplishments of the church as an organization and also of Christians in their personal and social lives. Many have realized their significance in the spirit of the service they give. This active spirituality moved people from their prayer closets to being present in many other capacities in their communities.

Notes

1. Parker J. Palmer, *Let Your Life Speak: Listening for the Voice of Vocation* (San Francisco: Jossey-Bass, 2000), 16.

2. *Saint Augustine: Confessions,* trans. Henry Chadwick (New York: Oxford University Press, 1991), 3.

3. James C. Anyike, *Historical Christianity: African Centered* (Chicago: Popular Truth, 1994).

4. "Religious orders (generally Catholic) use the word *charism* to describe their spiritual orientation and any special characteristics of their mission or values that might be exhibited as a result of the vows that they have taken and the orientation of the order to which they belong. An example might be the works of a teaching order as compared with that of a missionary order or one devoted to care for the poor or the sick." *Wikipedia,* s.v. "Charism," accessed July 29, 2014, http://en.wikipedia.org/wiki/Charism.

5. *Catholic Encyclopedia,* St. Clare of Assisi, www.newadvent.org/cathen/04004 a.htm. Accessed August 5, 2014.

6. Richard Rohr, *Eager to Love: The Alternative Way of Francis of Assisi* (Cincinnati: Franciscan Media, 2014), 522.

7. Keith Douglass Warner, OFM, "The Retrieval of a Distinctly Franciscan Spirituality and Intellectual Tradition," https://stfrancis.clas.asu.edu/sites/default/files/warner.pdf.

8. *Guidelines for the Development of the Franciscan Person,* Franciscan Federation, Rule and Life Committee, Washington, DC, 2008, 8, http://franfed.com/DevOfFran Per%20-%20Pages'08.pdf.

9. Ibid., 8.

10. Ibid., 9.

11. Ibid., 10.

12. Ibid., 12.

13. Ann Bezzerides, "Saints or Communists? Educating Orthodox Christian Youth for Love of the Neighbor," *Sophia*, vol. 2, 2010, 311.

14. Ibid., 321.

15. John Couretas, "Conflicted Hearts: Orthodox Christians and Social Justice in an Age of Globalization," www.orthodoxytoday.org/articles8/Couretas-Orthodox-Christianity-and-Globalization, Feb. 17, 2008.

16. This quote is attributed to St. John Chrysostom (C. 347–407 A.D.), *On Wealth and Poverty*, p. 55, SVS, Crestwood, NY, 1984) accessed at www.focusoc.org/index.php?option=com_content&view=article on August 5, 2014.

17. John Calvin, quoted in Howard L. Rice, *Reformed Spirituality: An Introduction for Believers* (Louisville: Westminster John Knox, 1991), 201.

18. William Brackney, "Baptists and Transformation: American Baptist Contributions," an Address Presented to the General Board of the American Baptist Churches, USA on the Anniversary of the Baptist Movement, 1609–2009. The paper was distributed to the members of the General Board.

19. Ibid.

20. Ibid.

21. Parker J. Palmer, *Let Your Life Speak: Listening for the Voice of Vocation* (San Francisco: Jossey-Bass, 2000), 3.

22. www.salvationarmyusa.org/usn/history-of-the-salvation-army.

23. Ibid.

24. www.salvationarmy.org/ihq/vision.

25. Ibid.

26. Center for Spiritual Life Development, www.salvationarmyspirituallife.org.

27. David Werner, "John Wesley's Question: 'How Is Your Doing?'" *Asbury Journal* 65, no. 2 (2010): 68–93.

28. C. Eric Lincoln and Lawrence H. Mamiya, *The Black Church in the African American Experience* (Durham, NC: Duke University Press Books, 1990), 47. The quote from John H. Satterwhite was taken from an unpublished background paper prepared for "The Black Church in the African American Experience" research project, 29.

29. Theophus H. Smith, "The Spirituality of Afro-American Traditions," in *Christian Spirituality: Post-Reformation and Modern. Series: World Spirituality: An Encyclopedic History of the Religious Quest*, Vol. 18; eds. Louis Dupre and Don E. Saliers (New York: Crossroad, 1989), 406.

30. Gayraud Wilmore, quoted in Smith, "The Spirituality of Afro-American Traditions," 406.

31. Ibid.

32. William Clemmons, "Protestant Spirituality: The Puritans and The Quakers," taken from his lecture presented for a course in Spiritual Direction for Evangelicals, Warrenville, IL, June 12, 1995.

33. C. Eric Lincoln and Lawrence H. Mamiya, *The Black Church in the African American Experience* (Durham, NC: Duke University Press Books, 1990), 165.

34. William Clemmons, "Protestant Spirituality: The Puritans and The Quakers," taken from his lecture presented for a course in Spiritual Direction for Evangelicals, Warrenville, IL, June 12, 1995.

35. C. Eric Lincoln and Lawrence H. Mamiya, *The Black Church in the African American Experience*, 165.

36. Theodore Walker Jr., *Empower the People: Social Ethics for the African American Church* (Maryknoll, NY: Orbis, 1991), 8.

37. Ibid., 9.

38. "The Story of Joanna P. Moore," American Baptist Historical Society, October 2, 2009, http://www.youtube.com/watch?v=h7W5gb_SgGY.

39. This information was gathered from the website of the American Baptist Home Mission Societies, www.abhms.org/come_from.cfm.

40. History-Legacy-Advocacy Information adapted from the website www.national baptist.com/departments/womans-auxiliary/history.html.

41. Ibid.

42. Bettye Collier-Thomas, *Jesus, Jobs, and Justice: African American Women and Religion* (New York: Alfred A. Knopf, 2010), 121.

CHAPTER 5

From Prayer Closet
to Food Pantry, from
Asceticism to Activism

From the seventeenth to the twentieth centuries, astute
leaders sought to extend the vision of the Christian life
beyond mere institutional participation.

—Brian McLaren[1]

Activism needs service in order to stay grounded and
remain connected to the needs and interests of people
experiencing the brunt of injustice. Service needs activism,
because without it, service can lead to dependency, failing
to address the root causes of neglect and need.

—Adam Russell Taylor [2]

Our Christian spirituality calls for us to bring our faith to action in transformative engagement. To be transformative we have to be involved
over the course of our lives in accomplishing God's purpose in the
earth—sharing the good news of Jesus Christ, showing compassion and
loving-kindness, sharing generously, and being others-centered with
active concern "for the least of these." We can find a pointed statement
of mission in Luke 4:18, where Jesus announces his ministry: "The
Spirit of the Lord is on me, because he has anointed me to proclaim

good news to the poor. He has sent me to proclaim freedom for the prisoners and recovery of sight for the blind, to set the oppressed free, to proclaim the year of the Lord's favor."

Sustained engagement is what has brought about the transformation we have seen over the centuries through the many Christian traditions as discussed in chapter 4. Bringing faith to social issues means more than engaging in general works of social activism, however. Social activism historically has been and is now a vital work of engagement that has brought about tremendous benefits to persons, societies, communities, and nations. The nature of social activism is rooted in our way of being. It is a faith witness, a faith practice that is distinguishable as spiritual activism, which carries a distinction of its own.

Our modern models discussed throughout this book have been examples of spiritual activism. Martin Luther King Jr., Dietrich Bonhoeffer, Fannie Lou Hamer, Dorothy Day, Jitsuo Morikawa, Shane Claiborne, Adam Taylor, and others not identified here are better understood as spiritual activists. They have worked from their prayer closets (their inner selves) to actualize their prayers through the outward works of food pantries, clothing banks, homes and shelters, schools, and peace houses. They have translated their asceticism in ways that speak loudly through their engagement in seeking sustainable solutions to issues of justice, equality, education, economic disparities, jobs, housing, and more. They have been activists.

So what is spiritual activism in the twenty-first century? We have seen and probably have participated in some form of spiritual activism ourselves. Today it shows up in the actions of the person who enlists in some local, national, or global drive for compassion and justice on behalf of society or of a group. It is demonstrated by the individual who is led to become a part of the solution to the needs that persist in our time. It is engaged in by the church, organization, club, or school that follows the call of Christ to be present and actively praying, doing, and being the love of God in places of need. It is not self-serving but is working for the betterment of others out of faithfulness to the call of God wherever and however that may be. As Dallas Willard explains social activism, "The true social activist is the person who lives as an apprentice of Jesus in his or her ordinary relationships."[3] The emphasis is on the heart or character of the believer.

Spiritual activists (and many reading these words may now identify themselves as such a person) find their significance as they are able to touch God's creation in a personal way. Through their churches, communities, workplaces, nonprofit ministries, and social agencies, they discover fulfillment in the relationships they engage in around myriad issues, and they find such engagements to be places of faithfulness. Spiritual activists unite with others when a call goes out or when an issue emerges in their neighborhoods or across the world. They may show up through acts of hands-on service, through acts of generosity in gifts or financial contributions, or through their prayers or presence. Spiritual activists are not looking for anything other than to serve God, be like Jesus, and obey the anointing of the Spirit to bring the Good News to the forefront through social transformation. These people live among us as ordinary faithful people who are passionate about compassion, righteousness, and justice. We can learn from the following models.

SPIRITUAL ACTIVISM
THROUGH LEADERSHIP

Marian Wright Edelman

Dr. Marian Wright Edelman was born during the time of the segregated South in Mississippi. She says that her inspiration came when she was a child watching what white children had the opportunity to do what she could not. Then she determined that she would have to grow up to change that. And that's just what she did. She graduated from Yale Law School and became the first African American to be licensed by the Mississippi Bar Association in 1963.

Dr. Wright Edelman joined the leadership of the modern civil rights movement, working under Martin Luther King Jr.'s leadership to advance justice and equality. Her life as an activist has been greatly focused on children. She was the founder of the Head Start program, and her social transformation as founder and president of the Children's Defense Fund is her great work and legacy. Today Dr. Wright Edelman says that she is calling for "a new transformation movement and it has to be about our children."[4]

Shane Claiborne

Shane Claiborne is a social activist, pastor, and author who chooses to live with the poor in a simple life of service. Shane cofounded and leads a fellowship of like-hearted activists who live together at The Simple Way, a Philadelphia-based community self-defined within a new monasticism as "a web of subversive friends conspiring to spread the vision of 'Loving God, Loving People, and Following Jesus' in our neighborhoods and in our world."[5] Shane's example of living an active faith defines spiritual activism at its best. His studies included sociology, youth ministry, and theology. However, the core of Shane's learning and the foundation of his work come from the words and works of Jesus in the Bible.

Shane Claiborne says, "I am convinced that the Christian Gospel has as much to do with this life as the next, and that the message of that Gospel is not just about going up when we die but about bringing God's Kingdom down. It was Jesus who taught us to pray that God's will be done 'on earth as it is in heaven.' On earth."[6] Shane is an influencer through his walk, word, and deed. He has taken the gospel and the model of Jesus seriously, developing model communities, like The Simple Way, that live out authentic radical discipleship indigenously every day. Shane is not only influencing the millennials and younger, but he is a relational thought partner with the baby boomer leaders, as well. He has coauthored a book with Dr. John Perkins titled *Follow Me to*

Freedom. This book is a must-read for anyone who wants to better understand the manner in which the two generations experience Christian social consciousness and perceive similarities and differences.

Adam Russell Taylor

Rev. Adam Russell Taylor has provided leadership to multiple organizations and institutions, including currently working at the World Bank as Lead, Faith-Based Initiative, External and Corporate Relations. In this capacity Adam leads the World Bank's outreach, partnership, and movement building efforts with faith-based organizations and communities.[7] Adam has served as vice president of advocacy at World Vision, a Christian humanitarian organization dedicated to working with children, families, and their communities worldwide to reach their full potential by tackling the causes of poverty and injustice. He served a yearlong fellowship in the White House Office of Public Engagement and Intergovernmental Affairs and was formerly the senior political director at Sojourners, where he was responsible for leading the organization in advocacy, coalition building, and constituency outreach.

The author of *Mobilizing Hope: Faith-Inspired Activism for a Post–Civil Rights Generation*, Taylor shares his journey and seeks to encourage emerging leaders. In a *Christianity Today* article titled "Faith Equals Action," Adam is reported as saying, "So much of why I care about social justice is because of my faith." He added, "My social and economic justice activism is rooted in trying to live out Jesus' call in Luke 4 to '"preach the good news to the poor . . . to release the oppressed, to proclaim the year of the Lord's favor."'"[8]

When asked how Christians are doing at being united around lifting people through economic justice, Taylor responded, "There has been a real shift in the American church, particularly among younger Christians engaging in social justice. Work needs to be done equipping young leaders with tools and skills in how to engage the political world.

A gap exists in the church between where opinion is and where action is. But there are lots of signs."[9]

Of course, there are many other model activists I could feature here, persons like Rev. Amy Butler, Rev. Jim Wallis, Rev. Al Sharpton, Rev. Barbara Clementine Harris, Rev. Dr. J. Alfred Smith Sr., Rev. Dr. Molly T. Marshall, Rev. Dr. Jacqueline Grant, Rev. Katie G. Cannon, Diana Hayes, Rev. Cheryl Townsend Gilkes, Rev. Dr. Emilie Townes, Rev. James Perkins, M. Shawn Copeland, William Sloane Coffin Jr., Ida B. Wells, Sojourner Truth, and many more in this century and the last.

May there be generations more who live to change the world by committing to follow Christ and be his witnesses.

Notes

1. Brian McLaren, *Finding Our Way Again: The Return of the Ancient Practices* (Nashville: Thomas Nelson, 2008), 53.

2. Adam Taylor, *Mobilizing Hope: Faith-Inspired Activism for a Post-Civil Rights Generation* (Downers Grove: IVP Books, 2010), 189.

3. Dallas Willard, quoted in James Bryan Smith, *The Good and Beautiful Community: Following the Spirit, Extending Grace, Demonstrating Love* (Downers Grove, IL: InterVarsity, 2010), 14.

4. Dr. Marian Wright Edelman made this comment during an interview aired on November 3, 2013 during the BET Black Girls Rock Awards Program, where she received a Social Humanitarian award.

5. www.thesimpleway.org/about.

6. Shane Claiborne, "What If Jesus Meant All That Stuff?" *Esquire*, www.esquire.com/features/best-and-brightest-20092009, November 18, 2009.

7. web.worldbank.org//TOPICS/CIVILSOCIETY. March 20, 2014.

8. Mark Moring and Tim Stafford, "Faith Equals Action," *Christianity Today*, January 2010, http:www.christianitytoday.com/ct/2010/January/31.80.html.

9. Ibid.

CHAPTER 6

Spirituality That Works: Contextual, Cultural, and in Community

The call to the way of discipleship is a call to belong to a community.
—Lawrence S. Cunningham and Keith J. Egan[1]

Remember: at the heart of this book is the message that spirituality brings an answer to the yearning for significance that is experienced by so many in our culture today. The connection between personal spirituality and social transformation makes living a significant life good discipleship. Individual disciplines and practices connect in practical and relevant ways to stir up, support, and sustain an active and engaged faith. The local church's work in disciple making is the practice of teaching people to carry kingdom principles like love of neighbor, justice, peace, mercy, and hope into their institutions, workplaces, communities, and so on. We are talking here about engaging your church through significant living, which is leading lives that serve.

Spirituality is contextual and cultural and is lived or expressed in community. A formative factor in the contextualization of spirituality provides grounding, a stabilizing force that provides a place to be and to serve. That, or those, contexts are immersed in culture, in ways and patterns of beliefs, perceptions, worldviews, acts, and behaviors. Culture makes up community, and community is beyond walls, surpassing boundaries of space and location, outside the limitations of geography, and leaping toward the commonalities of ideas, concerns, passions, and hopes. Spirituality that works is made visible as it is illuminated in context through culture and with community.

Context

Mission and ministry are centered in a context. As is popularly understood regarding the practice of theology, spirituality is also grounded in a context. Jesus' example demonstrates how we might respond to the call of our context. Throughout Jesus' earthly life he was engaged with his surroundings. His ministry was located in the cities, neighborhoods, marketplaces, synagogues, temples, homes, watering holes, countryside, mountains, valleys, lakes, rivers, and seas where he might have traveled or resided at any given time.

Six facets of context are pertinent for our discussion: geographic, social, economic, religious, demographic, and political. As we can note from both the biblical and contemporary models discussed in chapter 1, they lived deeply within their own contexts and responded to the situations and circumstances of their times. Focusing here on Jesus, we will see that he, too, responded to his various contexts.

Geographic

Following Luke's Gospel, we are informed that Jesus began his ministry in Galilee, which is said to have been a "center of change."[2] Galilee, by measures of ancient Israel, was a growing urbanized area. Jesus lived in Galilee, in the cities of Nazareth and the seaside town of Capernaum. As Jesus moved about from place to place, he was meeting the needs of those in circumstances around him. It was in these cities and in the nearby countryside that Jesus chose his disciples, healed, and taught. Galilee was the context within which Jesus lived and served. While localized there, certainly his impact is global.

A twentieth-century model, Martin Luther King Jr.'s geographical context was the American South, primarily Atlanta, Montgomery,

Birmingham, and Memphis. He was a Baptist preacher and a Southern leader. This was the locus of his movement, but the reach of his message, his actions, and his spirit was far wider. It was global. We can say that his geographic context was the United States, but his vision of justice and righteousness has reached across the oceans.

Social

Jesus, a young Jewish boy born in Bethlehem, was raised in Nazareth as the son of a carpenter who was likely of middle-class status. Nazareth was a small agricultural village with not much notable about it. People would have known each other. Remember the Scripture:

> Philip found Nathanael and told him, "We have found the one Moses wrote about in the Law, and about whom the prophets also wrote—Jesus of Nazareth, the son of Joseph."
> "Nazareth! Can anything good come from there?" Nathanael asked.
> "Come and see," said Philip. (John 1:45-46)

Seemingly insignificant social roots do not obstruct our capacity to live a life of significance, touching God's creation in a personal way.

Economic

Economic realities are incumbent in contexts. A context, whether urban or rural, institutional or familial, religious or secular, will have some economic nature. The notion of economy can be traced back to the Greek word *oikonomos* derived from *oikonom*, which carries the meaning of managing a house or "to manage," as in resources. Economics is defined as "the management of the resources, finances, income, and expenditure of a community, business enterprise, etc."[3]

When I look at the economies of my own context, I see my neighborhood's resources, which include not only its institutions, organizations, markets, and services, but also its people and their gifts, passions, labor, wills, interests, and concerns. With these latter resources per se, economy reaches far wider and with greater depth than if only income levels and money flow are considered. Economy goes far beyond dollars.

My grandmother, Big Mama (Irene B. Gardner), lived in rural Mississippi on farmland. She continued to plant and grow her own potatoes, greens, peas, beans, and such into her nineties. When the crops were ready, she harvested and stored what she needed for herself, but she would also load the trunk of her car with produce and drive to a nearby location and open the trunk for young families to come and take what they needed. This kept the young families fed and nourished. Big Mama and others like her were an integral part of that rural economy. Her care, her labor, her generosity, and her service boosted the quality of life of those who were recipients of her gifts. That economic gesture and many others like hers were a part of the character of that context.

Jesus demonstrated economy this way:

> As evening approached, the disciples came to him and said, "This is a remote place, and it's already getting late. Send the crowds away, so they can go to the villages and buy themselves some food."
>
> Jesus replied, "They do not need to go away. You give them something to eat."
>
> "We have here only five loaves of bread and two fish," they answered.
>
> "Bring them here to me," he said. And he directed the people to sit down on the grass. Taking the five loaves and the two fish and looking up to heaven, he gave thanks and broke the loaves. Then he gave them to the disciples, and the disciples gave them to the people. They all ate and were satisfied, and the disciples picked up

twelve basketfuls of broken pieces that were left over.
The number of those who ate was about five thousand
men, besides women and children. (Matthew 14:15-21)

Our ministry contexts operate within an economy that is able to sat-
isfy when we have the will to take what is there and who is there and join
with what God intends to do with us and through us.

Religious
"Preach the gospel at all times and when necessary use words."
These are the familiar words much attributed to Francis of Assisi. I
learned what is implied in these words when I went on a Franciscan
pilgrimage to Assisi with a group of education leaders. The embodiment of the gospel, of Jesus' character, was central to Francis's spirituality. To Francis, "preaching" the gospel was not something
reserved for sermons, homilies, or reflections. Preaching the gospel
was best to be seen, experienced, expressed, and embodied. So
much more than just religion, this type of "preaching" is in doing
and being. It is faith-engaged—faith that is not just belief but
action *present*.

So it is in this spirituality. Contextually it shows up in people who are
available to respond to the needs, concerns, and calling of God every
day anywhere. They are prepared to be the hands and feet of Christ
doing what God wants done in the world. James 2:18, 20-22 is a perfect
guide for us here:

> But someone will say, "You have faith; I have deeds."
> Show me your faith without deeds, and I will show you
> my faith by my deeds. . . .
> You foolish person, do you want evidence that faith
> without deeds is useless? Was not our father Abraham
> considered righteous for what he did when he offered his
> son Isaac on the altar? You see that his faith and his

actions were working together, and his faith was made complete by what he did.

Demographic

The demographics of an area are central to knowing the character, assets, needs, concerns, and affinity of the people who make up that context. The term *demography* means a description of people and is the study of population, trends, and movements. Demographic information comes from studying a particular population by looking at such things as age, race, gender, economic status, education levels, income levels, employment, and religious practices, among others. A local church must know the nature of their ministry context. Questions such as those below are important to ask.

1. What is the median age?
2. What is the average family size?
3. How many family households are there? How many single-person households? How many single-parent households? Single mothers? Multiple-generational households?
4. What is the median income?
5. What is the poverty rate within the census tract of the local church?
6. How many children under age twelve are in the community?
7. What is the percentage of retirees?
8. What is the percentage of persons who identify themselves as Christian? Muslim? Jewish? Hindu? Non-religiously affiliated?

Certainly having and interpreting data is helpful in framing some characteristics, assets, and needs of a context. But the best way to come to understand and know where you are doing ministry is to be engaged, to be present, and to be a "resident" with that community. A local church must see itself living among the neighbors who live outside of its doors, being concerned about that which they are concerned about, not a "them and us" but a sense of "we." This should be the case even as for many churches most of their membership may come from areas beyond the church's neighborhood. The local church also figures into the demographics of a context. Ask such questions as how many churches there are in a specific census tract, say a ten-block radius. What is the combined church membership of those persons who live within the census tract? Information such as this is readily available through the most recent US Census Report, or from your local governmental unit.

Data can indicate some areas for possible ministry, but a more personal way to discern and understand a service and ministry call is to know the people. Know the mothers, the fathers, the children and youth; know the schools, the administrators, the teachers and parents. You can develop relationships with local merchants, supporting them as appropriate with your business practices. Interact with city services, social justice organizations, and nonprofit and corporate leaders. Collecting one's own data by building relationships gives the local church firsthand demographic information that cannot be known by facts and figures alone.

Political

From the Greek word *politicos*, meaning "of, for, or relating to citizens," politics is the practice and theory of influencing other people on civic or individual levels. To go further with other definitions of *political* because it is important to have an understanding of how individuals interface with their particular political context, politics is also "of, relating to, or dealing with the structure or affairs of government, politics, or the state."[4]

Understanding that there is a political climate, a political culture, political norms, and political nuances within any given context is a valuable insight to possess as you intend to be engaged in your context and effect social transformation. The ability to influence the political process is a calling that many have responded to through public office and prophetic and transformational leadership. Others have been led to impact public policy by working to change policies that may have an adverse impact on those who are least able to pursue the vibrant and sustainable life that is expected in the United States or in global society.

American voting rights activist and civil rights leader Fannie Lou Hamer would walk into political rallies or meetings not just with a hymn in her heart but singing the hymn aloud. She believed that the civil rights movement was a matter of spiritual significance, not just civil action. She was a key leader of a political party, the Mississippi Freedom Democratic Party, which she served as vice chair. In this role she attended the 1964 Democratic National Convention.

The contemporary models discussed in earlier chapters—Morikawa, King, Hamer, Day, Bonhoeffer, Claiborne, and Taylor—all leveraged their persons, positions, and prophetic words to impact change and cause transformation as a matter of their callings and convictions and on behalf of community. For Dr. King it was the hope of a beloved community; for Dorothy Day the goal was for a more equitable community; for Fannie Lou Hamer it was a longing for a liberated community; for Jitsuo Morikawa the aim was an inclusive community; for Shane Claiborne it is simply community that reflects the kingdom of God here on earth.

Culture

Mission and ministry are grounded within culture. We all participate in customs, traditions, behaviors, and practices as members of communities, organizations, and institutions, including churches. Culture also varies globally—Eastern culture and Western culture, for example. Within the United States, cultural norms, assumptions, traditions, practices, behaviors, and perceptions vary from north to south to east to west. Nevertheless, I hasten to discourage any stereotyping. With the availability of technology, the Internet, and globalization of thoughts and ideas, culture cuts across boundaries of geography, age, race, ethnicity, language, and mobility. Therefore even the assumptions about culture itself must be tested against one's own experiences, observations, and relationships.

One example of culture is the professional business world, where value is placed on making contacts and networking. This is a perspective. To advance this perspective, professionals create business cards, which are products of such perspective. Professionals then share business cards with those they wish to be connected; thus that behavior becomes a practice. Perhaps business cards are then replaced with LinkedIn vCards. This cultural practice is attached to professional contexts. In more social contexts the practice is to request to be a Facebook "friend." Cultural practices are contextual.

Mission and ministry are practiced through and within culture or cultures. We experience more than one culture within a specific context. The shifting and mixing of cultures makes ministry more complex. In our time, a postmodern Christian era of post denominationalism and emerging-church culture, there is a need for a deeper understanding of cultural contexts.

Community

Mission and ministry are transformational in community. The word community is derived from the Latin word *communitatus*, which means fellowship, or *communis*, meaning common. There are many options for defining community. It is generally defined as a group of people living in the same locale sharing common interests, ideas, and values. Relatively new on the scene, Internet communities have no geographic boundaries but are communities of practice and interests. So when we speak of community and social transformation as it relates to social justice and the everyday lives of women, men, and children, we tend to be relating to the sense of holding things in common, whether in a specific geographic area or enhanced by the sharing that is enabled through the Internet.

Community is a structural design that God intended from the very beginning and exemplified throughout the biblical story. In fact, community can be seen from Genesis to Revelation. The Genesis story begins with what is understood as the community of God, including the Godhead with the heavenly beings. God then creates the community of humankind where earthly existence begins, and God intends companionship and fellowship to be the object of this creation. The aim of God's redemptive acts is to restore and maintain fellowship in community through the prophets, the apostles, the early church, and on into the new heaven and new earth.

Shane Claiborne writes:

> In fact the entire story of Jesus is about a God who did not just want to stay "out there" but who moves into the neighborhood, a neighborhood where folks said, "Nothing good could come. . . ." That is the God that we are just as likely to find in the streets as in the sanctuary, who can redeem revolutionaries and tax collectors, the oppressed and the oppressors . . . a God who is saving some of us from the ghettos of poverty, and some of us from the ghettos of wealth.[5]

Spirituality is not lived in isolation from the people around us. On the contrary, it leads us to be active in our community, expressing the love of God, answering the call of God to fulfill the purposes of God in our community and thus in the world. Walter Brueggemann addresses this in his book *Journey to the Common Good: Faith, Anxiety, and the Practice of Neighborliness*: "The great crisis among us is the crisis of 'the common good,' the sense of community solidarity that binds all in a common destiny—haves and have-nots, the rich and the poor." He further says, "We face a crisis about the common good because there are powerful forces at work among us to resist the common good, to violate community solidarity, and to deny a common destiny."[6] The church present in communities through work and service faces down such forces to advance the common good through a common faith.

VITAL SPIRIT, VITAL SERVICE

A blog post by a minister named Pastor Wayne, in which he discusses the local church's lack of engagement in the city and community that it is called to serve, says, "Go minister to the community and watch yourself build a church by accident. You see, Jesus is waiting on you to move so He can move and show Himself in your city. Stand up, leave your building, and go be a forerunner of Christ and reap a visitation of God in your city today."[7]

This spirituality is relevant, relational, and rejuvenating for the person, for the community, and for the church. The next chapter explores this further.

Notes

1. Lawrence S. Cunningham and Keith J. Egan, *Christian Spirituality: Themes from the Tradition* (New York: Paulist Press, 1996), ebook location 175.

2. Cynthia Astle, *Galilee in Jesus' Time Was a Center of Change: Herod Antipas' Building Schemes Urbanized a Rural Region*, http://ancienthistory.about.com/od/biblearchaeology/a/041511-CW-Galilee-In-Jesus-Time-Was-A-Center-Of-Change.htm

3. The Free Dictionary, www.thefreedictionary.com/economics.

4. *The American Heritage Dictionary of the English Language*, s.v. "political" (Boston: Houghton Mifflin, 2009).

5. Shane Claiborne, "What If Jesus Meant All That Stuff?" *Esquire*, www.esquire.com/features/best-and-brightest-2009, November 18, 2009.

6. Walter Brueggemann, *Journey to the Common Good Faith, Anxiety, and the Practice of Neighborliness* (Louisville: Westminster John Knox, 2010), 1.

7. Pastor Wayne is the pastor of Grace Point Church in McLoud, Oklahoma. Blog posting for June 26, 2011, http://www.gracepointlife.org/blog.

CHAPTER 7

Spirituality That Works:
Relevant, Relational,
and Rejuvenating

Don't ask what the world needs. Ask what makes you
come alive and go do it. Because what the world needs
are people who have come alive.

—Howard Thurman[1]

"What does the world need?" is an age-old question some have asked as
a way to discover how and where they might make a difference. Making
a difference is closely tied to the yearning for significance, but it is also
a concern that seeks relevance.

What does the world need? More teachers? More resources? More
technology? More peace? Perhaps the answer is in that popular 1965
song composed by Burt Bacharach and made famous by Dionne
Warwick: "What the world needs now is love, sweet love." However
prolific the question is in any generation, the answer (or answers) are
equally prolific.

Quite a challenge to us comes from the late theologian and educator
Howard Thurman through the epigraph above. According to Dr.
Thurman's statement, we are asking the wrong question. He says, "Ask
what makes you come alive and go do it. Because what the world needs
are people *who have come alive*" (emphasis added). In these few

words, the great spiritual thinker points us in the direction of Christian spirituality that is so relevant, relational, and deeply rejuvenating as to come alive. We'll look at each of these outcomes.

Spirituality That Works Is Relevant

What makes for something or someone to be relevant? How is relevance understood or identified today in our contexts or even in our culture? In a previous ministry context, working with college students, I had the opportunity to develop new programs that would help traditional undergraduates understand themselves more deeply and explore their sense of call, sense of service, and passion. Over the years, after hearing them speak their hearts and watching them as they showed excitement when they volunteered in a way that helped someone or some organization, I discovered that this generation has a deep passion for service. Consequently, I developed a pilot program that would give students a short-term internship experience working with a nonprofit agency in an urban setting and directly addressing a specific social issue.

While initially implemented as a summer experience, the pilot program resulted in a year-long placement of students in a single agency to add to the service capacity of the organization. Everyone involved in the program, from the students and the agency leaders to those in the target community, reflected that their experiences through the model had had a significant impact. This program became popular among both students and agencies as their experience was shared within the community. The resulting growth of the program came more by their testimony than by our solicitation. Through this experience, I gained an understanding that a high level of impact makes for relevant work.

Over recent years, before and since the new millennium, I have been a part of conversations about the postmodern era of the Christian church. In the age of the emerging church, I offer no clarity between emerging and existing; many other books have been written to do that. What I offer is the understanding that, by living a significant life through our spirituality and discipleship, we make a difference in the world that is relevant and impactful.

Spirituality That Works Is Relational

The very question concerning what the world needs is a relational one. It seeks to make some connection with and to achieve some knowledge or understanding about what is often simply referenced as "the world" when the object of the question generally means a focus on persons, groups of persons, society, or something that represents a realm that is larger than ourselves. Writer and theologian Frederick Buechner's popular quote gets at that dynamic: "The place God calls you to is the place where your deep gladness and the world's deep hunger meet."[2]

By this I connect the mutuality of the world's deep hunger with our deep gladness to be a place that is not just an *intersection* but the place for an *interaction*; an interaction, because when we engage persons, a community, a "world," the exchange is beneficial to us in meeting our need as it is hoped to be in having met the needs of others. In this, our service is a two-way street, mutually fulfilling a need.

We are not called to places of need without need of our own. Haven't you had someone ask you, "So, why did you do that?" and your response was, "Because I had the need to"? Sometimes that is the most honest response we can give: simply the need to. Remember the song mentioned earlier in the introduction:

> If I can help somebody, as I pass along,
> if I can cheer somebody with a word or song,
> if I can show somebody they are traveling wrong,
> then my living shall not be in vain.

If for no other reason, we have the need to fulfill our discipleship call to reach others for Christ. We have a need to show God's love in a world that has a great need for genuine demonstrations of gospel love.

We have the need to spread around our sense of "Jesus joy" that can only be accomplished in relationship with others. These relationships that evolve extend themselves into friendships in our lives.

In his book *Making Friends, Making Disciples: Growing Your Church through Authentic Relationships*, Lee Spitzer talks about the role the Christian church has played historically in creating communities of friendships: "The Christian church has led the way in creating community." He asks, " Can we discover a transformative paradigm for church growth—not only in terms of the number of people who join but also in regard to the maturity of disciples who participate in the life of the church?" Then he adds, "Friendship, community, discipleship, evangelism, and social witness all play starring roles in the church's fulfillment of God's will."[3]

More than the world's deep hunger getting fulfilled by our service, we receive a sense of connectedness, of relatedness, of friendship that touches us deeply, reaching our soul's core and bringing about great gladness.

Spirituality That Works Is Rejuvenating

The words of Revelation 3:1-2, "I know your deeds; you have the reputation of being alive, but you are dead. Wake up! Strengthen what remains and is about to die," and Howard Thurman's "Ask what makes you come alive and go do it. Because what the world needs are people who have come alive" are of the same spirit in instruction to us. Yes, what the world needs is people who have come alive, but I hasten to add that the church, the spiritual body of Christ, also needs people who have come alive. Can we draw as a logical conclusion then, that if we want a *world* that is alive, we must be a *church* that is alive? Would it also stand to reason that if we want a church that is alive, we must be disciples who are alive? If you want to be a disciple who is alive, then do what makes you come alive.

Let's further examine the scriptural words "you have the reputation of being alive." To understand this more clearly, what does it mean to be *alive*? Besides the obvious, that it means to have physical life with a beating heart and lungs that inhale and exhale, with a mind that processes the world in some meaningful way, *alive* carries the inference of being alert, animated, active, awake, sensitive, energetic, vigorous, spirited, and vital. There is this sense that *being alive* is to have an impact on one's surroundings. Such liveliness cannot be overlooked, missed, or unobserved.

An applicable example that comes to my mind is my two-year-old twin nephews. They define alertness for me in how they are aware of and responsive to the smallest thing in their surroundings. They recognize when something new has developed in the living room and quickly find their way to this new thing to examine it and explore the possible effect of its presence, to see if there is some usefulness in it–which translates into *Can we touch it? Eat it? Play with it?* and only rarely, *Should I be afraid of it?* While for intrepid two-year-olds, the question of fear is not the first thing on their minds, for adults, fear may be an early phase of inquiry.

President Barack Obama, in his speech during the Fiftieth Anniversary Commemoration of the March on Washington, referred to the students who were instrumental in the efforts of the movement during the 1960s. In pointing to the hope of our new generations, President Obama remarked, "The young are not constrained by habits of fear. They are willing to engage in the 'what ifs?'"[4]

As was mentioned in chapter 1, millennials present an opportunity for the church as well as a challenge, but a greater gift than challenge. The millennial and younger generations bring to the church, as President Obama said in his commemoration speech, "the hunger of purpose."[5]

"You have the reputation of being alive." The church has had a reputation over the centuries for liveliness. In many ways across the globe, the church has been at the forefront of making true the gospel and the works of righteousness and justice. Baptist, and in particular American Baptist, contributions are clear examples of aliveness through their roles in theological, social, and political transformation.

Walter Rauschenbusch (1861–1918) was one chief contributor. William Brackney writes in his essay "Baptists and Transformation: American Baptist Contributions" of Rauschenbusch who "rose from a humble pastoral role in a ghetto of sorts in New York's Lower East Side to become one of the world's great social theorists and Christian transforming agents." Brackney references Rauschenbusch's book *A Theology of the Social Gospel* (1917), which "became a theological classic, republished in several languages." Students of Rauschenbusch's thinking included Howard Thurman, Martin Luther King Jr., Helen Barrett Montgomery, and even the former head of Christian Aid in Great Britain, Michael Taylor.[6]

Most commonly, social transformation occurs as any person, group, institution, or organization acts in ways to bring about change in the order of things, situations, circumstances, policies, or practices. For example, Sister Simone Campbell and the League of Catholic Women Religious (LCWR) were participants of the "Nuns on the Bus" movement of 2010–12. They leaned on their commitment to Catholic social teaching and their own adherence to the gospel as their mandate to protest what they considered to be an unjust US federal budget proposed by Congressman Paul Ryan. It seemed to me that their witness and demand for a "faithful budget" awakened many others to take interest in this particular proposal's potential impact on poor people in the United States.

It isn't just politics when clergy meet with the president of the United States to discuss immigration reform or when Christian coalitions press their state legislators for stronger gun control. Every day, ordinary people awake to the call of God's purpose and make choices motivated by their love of Christ and expressed as serving as his hands and feet.

Living church is real. Dwight Stinnett, editor of the Living Church series, encourages the church to reject any impending sense of demise and to see that the church *is* alive because God is still working through the church. When we live from the basis of our spirituality—our internal God connection—engaged and concerned about that which God is concerned about, our living has greater meaning. Our life is of greater consequence and purpose. We are important to our world *because what the world needs are people who have come alive.*

Notes

1. Howard Thurman, quoted in Gil Bailie, *Violence Unveiled: Humanity at the Crossroads* (New York: Crossroad, 1995), xv.

2. Frederick Buechner, *Wishful Thinking: A Theological ABC* (New York: Harper and Row, 1973), xii.

3. Lee B. Spitzer, *Making Friends, Making Disciples: Growing Your Church through Authentic Relationships*, Living Church, ed. Dwight J. Stinnett (Valley Forge, PA: Judson, 2010), ix.

4. President Barack Obama, speech delivered at the Fiftieth Anniversary Commemoration of the March on Washington, August 28, 2013.

5. Ibid.

6. William H. Brackney, "Baptists and Transformation: American Baptist Contributions," paper presented during the meeting of the General Board of the American Baptist Churches USA, 2009.

CHAPTER 8

Learning from One Another

They gave offerings of whatever they could—far more
than they could afford!—pleading for the privilege of
helping out in the relief of poor Christians. This was
totally spontaneous, entirely their own idea, and caught
us completely off guard. What explains it was that they
had first given themselves unreservedly to God and to us.
The other giving simply flowed out of the purposes of
God working in their lives.

—2 Corinthians 8:3-5, MSG

In living lives of significance through spirituality and service, we can discover what makes for best practices and lessons to be learned from
churches and church leaders. Very little needs to be invented or newly
designed in order to do ministry that touches God's creation in a personal way. In 2 Corinthians 8 the Macedonian church was ministering
not out of their wealth but out of their poverty. The church had fallen
on hard times financially. But as Paul put it in verse 2 (MSG), "The trial
exposed their true colors: They were incredibly happy, though desperately poor. The pressure triggered something totally unexpected: an
outpouring of pure and generous gifts."

We first learn from this biblical model that the spirit of service
and engagement to alleviate the needs of others can be motivated
by the church's own great need. They found deep gladness while

meeting a great need. They received "Jesus joy" in the midst of their own trials.

When we act as a learning community, many effective ministry models can bring understandings that demonstrate fundamental principles useful to churches. It is vital to strengthen or establish discipleship ministries that offer the church a way to support members as they engage in their context through a bold expression of their spirituality at work.

Ministry Models That Work

Through the following exemplary ministries, I have identified a particular method or ministry stream that supports and sustains the transformative work that each is called to. From each example, I have identified that strength. Taken together or separately, these ministry methods form ministry principles that can be applied within other church contexts. The principles will be discussed in chapter 9, but here I have labeled each ministry model by what stands out as one of the church's specific tactics.

Model for Legacy Leaders	Calvary Baptist Church, Milwaukee, Wisconsin
Model for Parish Engagement	All Saints Catholic Church, Milwaukee, Wisconsin
Model for Servant Leadership	The Church of the Saviour, Washington, DC
Model for Spiritual Formation	First Corinthian Baptist Church, Harlem, New York
Model for Collective Activism	Housing Ministries of American Baptists in Wisconsin

MODEL FOR LEGACY LEADERS
Calvary Baptist Church, Milwaukee, Wisconsin

Is it possible for God to have a specific call to a specific church and for God's hand to be seen in bringing church and pastor together for a life-long presence in a specific ministry? Given the story of Calvary Baptist Church in Milwaukee, Wisconsin, I believe the possibility is real. Sometimes there is a stream of pastoral leaders whose calls and passions align with a continuum of God's mission for a church. And at other times there are legacy churches whom God has given sustained prophetic missions and through whom God extends visionary calls to leadership—the leadership of legacy ministries.

Calvary Baptist Church was the first African American Baptist church in the city of Milwaukee, founded in 1895. Milwaukee was just fifty years old at that time. The primary neighborhoods where the African American community settled were also the areas where the first churches were established. The mission of Calvary Baptist Church was to minister to African American, urban, lower- to-middle-class professionals and blue-collar workers.

Calvary Baptist, a church with a rich heritage and significant legacy, is the mother church for many Baptist churches in Milwaukee. The first African American business owner in Milwaukee was a member of this church, as were the first African Americans to found and own a savings and loan company. Other firsts from this congregation were the first African American public school teacher, lawyer, judge, and physician. During the city's civil rights movement, the pastor, Rev. Walter B. Hoard, became the president of the local branch of the NAACP.

This church has been the home church of state representatives, a state senator, the city treasurer of Milwaukee, and the first clergy-woman to serve as president of the American Baptist Churches USA (in 2000).

Calvary suffered damages to its choir stand when the church was fire-bombed following a NAACP rally. This incident was significant in solid-ifying the church's understood role in Milwaukee and the church's surrounding community. A case in point was when the time came for the church to discern where it would build a new church building. The decision was made to remain and build within the central city, a decision that arose from the church's understanding of God's purpose. Not only was that decision defining for its mission and ministry, but it was also defining for the unique pastoral leader the church would call.

Seven pastors have served at Calvary since its founding. Calvary has sought God's guidance on each pastoral call, and each call has been extended to someone with an awareness that the church has embraced their call to be spiritually active in addressing the spiritual, social, physical, and economic realities of not only their parishioners but of the community as well.

While one pastor served as president of the NAACP, the succeeding pastor was elected alderman and served as a voice for the poor and the oppressed in the community. One pastor planted the vision of a church that would be strategically located within a community that needed their ministry and whose residents were theirs to disciple and shepherd. The next pastor began implementing a vision to develop the area surrounding the church with the resources the community most desperately needed. This vision included housing for the elderly and physically challenged, an economic development project, a community center for youth and families, stores and shops, and a school.

The housing developments were launched in 1975, and the church approached the Department of Housing and Urban Development (HUD) for funding. It was at this time that Congress had placed a moratorium on new construction and funding contracts. A ministry partner, Rev. Carmen Porco, executive director of Housing Ministries of American Baptists in Wisconsin, set up a meeting with the US senator representing Wisconsin to begin lobbying Congress and HUD to lift the moratorium. In the end, the moratorium was lifted enough to grant funding to the church's new development arm to develop seventy-two apartments on land that was purchased adjacent to the church building. This was a major breakthrough that the church knows was a result of prayer, purpose, and partnership. Since then two other apartment complexes have been built.

The vision for the second phase established an economic development project. The community development arm of the church established a bindery business that trained and employed persons from the community. While this phase was not sustained, the housing ministry has survived, largely using the expertise and leadership from members of the church. The pastor during that time, Rev. Dr. Roy B. Nabors, was eventually elected to the Common Council and served as a pastor and governmental official.

The season of activist pastoral leadership was followed by a season of inward spiritual growth, with a focus on strong preaching, fervent prayer, and expanded study under the leadership of Rev. Tommie L. Mims. Could it be that this interlude that saw a three-year ministry of inward focus was what God instituted for this historic church to help it to remain spiritually strong for the future work that God would call them to? The church has described that era as a time in their congregational life that felt like how it must have been when Jesus went to the garden to pray, or out into the boat, or to the mountain where his transfiguration took place. It would be the next pastor who would work to expand the leadership and collaborative reach into the interfaith community through building common ground and collective action, coupled with strengthening Christian education and discipleship ministries along with spiritual gift development.

Rev. Dr. James E. Leary served Calvary for eighteen years, from the mid-1980s through the early 2000s. The prophetic and activist leadership that was the mark of Calvary continued. Leary was a preacher of liberation theology, social justice, and spiritual activism, and during his pastorate, Calvary's spiritual preparation for an activism ministry was deepened. Leary focused on ministries that empowered laypersons to live from the inside out. His signature ministry was the development of the spiritual gifts ministry. Calvary members administered the spiritual gifts assessment to all current leaders, prospective leaders, and the general membership. Understanding one's gifts became the entry into discerning ministry and mission callings and engagement. Parishioners were also supported and encouraged in fulfilling their gifts and callings in their workplaces and family life. Through Leary's affiliation with the Gamaliel Foundation, he became a cofounder and founding president of the Milwaukee Inner City Congregations Allied for Hope (MICAH). The Gamaliel Foundation is a grassroots network of non-partisan, faith-based organizations that empower ordinary people to effectively participate in the political, environmental, social, and economic decisions affecting their lives.

Calvary became one of the founding churches of MICAH along with more than one hundred others in central city Milwaukee. Pastors and congregants join together to address the issues of poverty, education, crime, illegal drug use, housing, and more.

The current pastor, Rev. Dr. John R. Walton Jr., stands in the shoes of his predecessors, perpetuating the vision of transforming the community for Christ. Reverend Walton strongly believes that God sent him to Calvary Baptist Church so that he can continue the legacy of the vision to develop the complete square-block radius around the church to grow an inner-city campus that will serve the community through housing, education, economic development, and a community center that includes a health clinic and training center for youth. Says Reverend Walton, "We are going to need a facility with an indoor track to encourage wellness where it is a safe environment. We need a place for kids to skate, run about, play, and learn. These ways of serving or ministering to the community arise from the realities of an urban church with the particularities in the Calvary demographic. For example, the high rate of teen pregnancies gives rise to needs for children and young mothers. Thus the vision for a school that accepts children from zero to five years old is to give children a strong education and a spiritual and safe place to grow during the early formative years. We will further meet the need for health and wellness by providing a clinic for prenatal care." (The quotes in this section are from a personal interview on September 13, 2013.)

This vision and the disciple-making ministry of the church are supported through a four-point model for empowerment that includes preaching, teaching, pastoral care, and fellowship. Reverend Walton emphasizes that how people see "themselves has an effect on discipleship and the sense of opportunity and ability for one to contribute to the good of others." If there is a "very strong sense of apathy," then convincing the people that they can be used by God to bring the shift to their communities through service and servant leadership is a challenge and an opportunity. Citing a statement from Marvin McMickle's book *Preaching to the Black Middle Class*, Reverend Walton continues with the point that the urban preacher's challenge is convincing the persons who have means and capacity to give in support of a neighborhood and/or community that they have a call or responsibility to do so.

"Our seven points of vision include helping people who are hurting, confused, lonely, and depressed, and we try to disciple people to make themselves available to God. So, here I am." Reverend Walton declares, "I have found my purpose here with this ministry. I sense the anointing on my life for ministry and this vision here at Calvary."

He continues, "When you leave on Sunday, the worship experience fuels you, but you don't leave God; you leave to worship God. The spiritual disciplines and worship are a lifestyle. You may find that you practice only three of [Richard] Foster's identified spiritual disciplines, but you do those three."

Reverend Walton finds that building a network and a partnership base as a key strategy for the church to build on invites others who share the vision and who hold a piece of its implementation. He sees this as a strong step he is taking to empower the church and equip them to transform the community for Christ.

MODEL FOR PARISH ENGAGEMENT
All Saints Catholic Church, Milwaukee, Wisconsin
All Saints Catholic Church is a central city Milwaukee parish and is notable for an array of significant ministries. As a merger of many

parishes located in a largely African American area of Milwaukee, the All Saints congregation embodies the diverse breadth of the body of Christ. Members and visitors enjoy it for its diversity.

The church edifice expresses the dominant culture that is Africentric. Hanging within the edifice is a freedom quilt commemorating the Freedom Road of Southern slaves through the Underground Railroad; it was designed by a parish member and fabricated by others. The liturgy, with its finest rendering of music, from traditional hymns to the best in gospel and contemporary praise and worship, is a vibrant reflection of the people. The church's pastor, Fr. Carl Diederichs, can be heard proclaiming the gospel and strong Catholic social teachings through homilies that emphasize the call to a discipleship that seeks justice and serves the poor.

You would expect such from a church whose mission reads:

We, members of All Saints Catholic Church, commit ourselves with the help of God to:

■ Bring the Good News of Christ to the people of Milwaukee's central city and beyond,

■ Work for justice for the poor and the powerless,

■ Continue to build up and foster a multi-racial, multi-cultural community of faith, hope and love,

■ Celebrate the Death and Resurrection of Jesus in Word and Eucharist (www.allsaintsmke.com)

Currently, All Saints has five community outreach programs:

■ the Commons, a home for homeless women and children;

■ an afterschool mentoring program for youth;

■ the nightly meal program;

■ the food pantry, which provides nutritious meals and food to families in need; and

■ an emergency assistance program called the Ujima Project.

Father Carl says, "As people who are baptized, we claim by our baptism that we are priests, we're prophets, we are royalty, and we're servant leaders, and from that reality the very first thing that we would do then is to look to the needs of others. Financial needs, physical needs, their need for housing, their needs for food, just for love and concern—we are there for that." (The quotes in this section are from a personal interview on September 17, 2013)

The priest continues, "Just look at what people can actually do. Just this one little parish, All Saints, feeds 128 people three nights a week. We give food out twice a week to hundreds of people. We have homeless women and children living in a wonderfully decent place with food. There are women in the Commons who are not going to return to the street. They're not going to return to poverty because we've given them enough cushion so that they can go to school or get another job. Just staying within the church's geographical context—what if other churches did this? What if every parish had a home for homeless women and children? Now, if others were to do that, we could solve this thing [homelessness.]

"I would like to focus on this parish as a whole, living, Catholic, Christian community," Father Carl explains, "a community in love with our God and in love with each other. And from there the community outreach work organically flows. We are a beacon for the poor, the spiritually and corporally needy, and the dispossessed."

Spiritual formation for the members is engaged in an inward/outward spirituality that is active and serving. How can a pastor with a limited budget and with a staff that is part-time focus on what would make a difference? "One way is the intergenerational Festival of Faith. It is not the old Sunday school model. It is the model for faith formation that is a six-year cycle. Social justice is a theme for six sessions. Another is the liturgical piece—the Rite of Christian Initiation (RCI). Basically it is the catechumen. Lastly, it is the Sunday liturgies, which are a deep exposure to lots of Scriptures. Then we are ready for the outreach. It is not the personal spirituality; it is an outward service that is not done on your own but is done with others. We stress that as a Christian you are not serving as a volunteer. You are there by rite and by right. Sociologically, a volunteer is someone who is in and out. A person who is there to serve by way of calling is there to make the difference. You can proliferate programs but not with a limited budget. So we focus on what is essential. Then there is just life—observe, judge, act. You see the needs, you ask how you can affect the need, then you pray and you act accordingly. The mistake is to think that a parish must go it alone. But that is not the call. We collaborate. We work in partnerships with others. We cast the net and seek others to assist us, or we assist them. We serve the 128 meals three times a week with the help of other parishes who come, serve, and contribute food. It is a way to meet the needs of many not dependent on or limited by your budget." The people who come to help with the meal will not only serve, but they will eat with the people to share stories, hear their stories, and form relationships.

Spiritual activism for Father Carl is based on Matthew 25 and the model of St. Vincent de Paul. According to Father Carl, St. Vincent de Paul rejected the rigid, commandment-based, purist spirituality and started a group called "oratory." The group lived a prayer practice that held that when you're in prayer and someone comes to the door in need, you go to the need; you are still in the moment present in prayer. Father Carl explains, "When the call comes you answer. There is an urgency to answer the call. You are then in God's will for you at that moment when you are helping another. Then the heart is connected with what the hand is to do."

When asked how he encourages his parishioners to maintain balance between their active Christian service and the contemplative life, Father Carl points to their practice of having the parish members sign a Member Covenant annually (adapted from the Church of the Saviour model; see page 109). This covenant supports the members' commitment to the spiritual disciplines that will sustain them and support them in their lives and service, as well as in their commitment to engage in

Christian service and work in the outward acts of the church and their faith. It reads as follows:

All Saints Catholic Church Member Covenant[1]

As a new member of All Saints Catholic Church (and continuing member), I pledge:

- To pray for the members of All Saints daily,
- To participate in ongoing faith formation for myself and family,
- To worship with the family of All Saints at least weekly,
- To participate actively in the liturgical/prayer-life of the Church as a liturgical minister,
- To participate actively in the Outreach Ministries of All Saints or in a ministry in the larger community,
- To contribute to the financial well-being of All Saints regularly.

With the grace of God, I now sign this Covenant as I begin my membership (and continue) within the Beloved Community of All Saints.

Signature

Explaining the All Saints practice of prayer, Father Carl says, "I use and lead persons in a Centering Prayer process. I encourage ten minutes in the morning, ten minutes at night. Start with Lectio Divina and then you keep the ten minutes no matter how pulled you are. Be there and be present. Stay there. It gives you the ability to respond to the ways you are challenged day to day that is faithful and consistent with your faith and life."

Father Carl further explains, "If I'm known as somebody who loves and cares for the poor and not in just some pure and saccharine way but in a way that it hits my own pocketbook, then I've done, I think, the kind of servant leadership that ordination calls me to do." He continues, "I want to be seen as somebody who truly does care about the very people that Jesus cared about and as somebody who is willing to pay the price for doing this. That would be the end of the story."[2]

The All Saints parish website issues this invitation to anyone: "Our doors are open. Come join us in worship and in service." What strikes me about this invitation is that you can always expect a church website to invite persons to join them in worship, but rarely have I seen that it would also say "and in service."

MODEL FOR SERVANT LEADERSHIP
The Church of the Saviour, Washington, DC

I am profiling The Church of the Saviour in Washington, DC, because of their deep and unique form of Christian activism. "Activist DC church" is how the *Washington Post* described the Church of the Saviour in its article about the church's ministry.[3] The Church of the Saviour is a multiracial, ecumenical, social justice-oriented, faith-based activist faith community (or communities) in Washington, DC. The church's founders, Gordon Cosby (d. 2013) and Mary Campbell Cosby, had a desire to be part of a disciplined, committed, diverse, ecumenical church. This style of church is what the Cosbys led to full development after Gordon Cosby returned to the States after serving in military chaplaincy in 1946. One look at the church's organizational structure, if it can be called one, will soon disclose that this is no ordinary traditional church. This makes them most intriguing and, yes, very radical.

A powerful telling of the church's history is available on their website (www.inwardoutward.org) and is worthy of reading. But most important for the purposes of our learning from The Church of the Saviour is the life balance that the Cosbys led the church into develop-ing, which they call the Inward/Outward Journey. The church mem-bers are strategically aligned to live out a radical activist faith and a liv-ing display of the gospel as they imitate the life of Jesus Christ as true disciples and persons of the Way.

Members are called to be engaged in outward actions and activities that seek to pursue justice and peace and show love to all people. Yet they are also led in an inward focus to slow themselves from busyness and to be in an inner relationship with God. This is accomplished through providing quiet spaces, silent retreats, prayerful reflections, and regularity in worship and stewardship.

The Inward/Outward Tradition

The focus on the inner life toward a deeper love and relationship with God, with oneself, and with others is at the core of the way at The Church of the Saviour. But equally so are the discernment and growth in understanding and fulfilling the calling of each person to be engaged in active ministry and mission. This position of the church has resulted in a bountiful array of ministries that reach deeply into communities. The ministries have grown out of the faithful adherence to the ministry model that all are called to service and to commit to responding to the issues and needs that affect the vulnerable, marginalized, oppressed, and poor.

The Churches

The structure of the community at The Church of the Saviour is impor-tant to note, while it also may not be easy to describe. The structure, in my opinion, gives opportunity to the ministry of the church, or I should say churches. The ministry began in 1946 with one church; however, today there are nine churches within The Church of the Saviour com-munity, plus four affiliated communities.

These churches, said to be comprised of "ordinary" people, began as small mission groups who came together around identified and specific mission interests within neighborhoods and communities and around particular social issues. The Church of the Saviour is self-described as a "scattered community" of small independent churches. (There is much more to be said about how these churches and The Church of the Saviour function, so I urge you to visit their website for greater depth: www.inwardoutward.org/the-church-of-the-saviour/churches.)

Member Formation

The formation of members of these churches is intentional and formal. Each member takes classes in the church's School of Christian Living or the Servant Leadership School. This period of formation is generally one to three years. Following this experience, members discern their continuation on an annual basis, renewing their commitment and call to walk in the way of the life and practices of the church.

The church's practice of inward life, reflection, prayer, and spiritual practices are balanced by the emphasis on maintaining the outward life, or service. The outward life is developed through training in the School of Servant Leadership. When I attended my first Servant Leadership conference, I became aware of the approach of this church and their School of Servant Leadership. I heard more about them seven years later while attending another conference. I was very impressed and intrigued. Their model has remained in the forefront of my mind.

The mission of the Servant Leadership School is theological education emphasizing an intersection of spirituality and social justice. Servant leadership as a practice, a way of life, or as a discipline is akin to Jitsuo Morikawa's view that all persons are called to live out their faith in service to others in all aspects of their lives, but particularly in their workplaces.

The school's curriculum and training are inclusive of both spiritual and social practices. There are six pillars around which the teaching takes place: call in community, prayer and contemplation, Scripture and the Christian tradition, economic and earth justice, liberation from oppression, and peace and reconciliation. Through these themes, we can see the inward/outward tradition, which is strictly adhered to as commitment to a way of Christian life that marks the students as followers of Jesus Christ and doers of his mission to restore and reclaim God's creation.

MODEL FOR SPIRITUAL FORMATION
First Corinthian Baptist Church, Harlem, New York

First Corinthian Baptist Church of New York is located in Harlem at 1912 Adam Clayton Powell Jr. Boulevard. Rev. Michael A. Walrond Jr. serves as the seventh senior pastor of this historic church. He is a graduate of Morehouse College and holds a master of divinity degree from Duke Divinity School. Pastor Walrond, or "Pastor Mike," as he is called by parishioners, is a church leader, a social justice and social transformation prophet, a respected civic leader, and a visionary builder.

The church's mission is "Making disciples to transform the world,"[4] and their vision statement reads, "We are an ever-evolving community of visionaries and dreamers who have been called by God to live the lives we were created to live, commanded by God to love beyond the limits of our prejudices and commissioned by God to serve!" Even a quick look at their website reveals that this approach to ministry and making disciples is focused on a spirituality that works.

First Corinthian has an extensive spiritual formation ministry. The 2013 course catalog is titled "Season of Awakening. Life Is Calling." The catalog opens with these words: "FCBC's Spiritual Formation program helps participants in clarifying and defining their journey as disciples of Jesus. Avid readers and newbies benefit greatly through the shared readings and discussions via Bible Basics, Discipleship Training Classes, and an array of other offerings." These course offerings say a lot about how the church understands its context, leverages culture, and designs community.

I am highly impressed by the strong focus on spiritual formation at First Corinthian Baptist. Spiritual formation is central to developing leaders, disciples, and visionaries who will lead from their faith and their knowledge. I have chosen to focus on this part of the ministry at First Corinthian because I have always believed spiritual formation and discipleship training are ministries that undergird and support, not only calling and service, but also all other ministries of the church. The courses and materials used at the time of this writing are shared below. They are Bible Basics, Political Formation, Gender Awareness, Spirituality, and Ministerial Leader Formation.

Bible Basics
The Bible Basics course uses a book by Erwin Raphael McManus, *The Barbarian Way: Unleash the Untamed Faith Within*, and the course description reads: "This course will help you unleash the untamed faith within: *The Barbarian Way*. Two thousand years later the call to follow Jesus lacks risk, passion, and sacrifice. Is this really what Jesus died for? Jesus never made a pristine call to a proper or safe religion. Jesus beckons His followers to a path that is far from the easy road."

In *The Barbarian Way*, McManus encourages us to consider the bold and risky life of Jesus' disciples that is evident in the Bible, a call to "fight for the heart of your King!"[5] McManus illustrates this bold, barbarian way of being and doing historically. He says, however, of today's church:

> Christianity over the past two hundred years has moved from a tribe of renegades to a religion of conformists. Those who choose to follow Jesus become participants in an insurrection. To claim we believe is simply not enough. The call of Jesus is one that demands action.[6]

This view of the barbarian way of actively living out a calling as the presence of Christ in our communities very concretely demands a spirituality that works. It is a vital spirit displayed in vital service.

Another course offered in Bible Basics uses Howard Thurman's book *Jesus and the Disinherited*.[7] This Bible Basics offering is described like this:

> The course will focus on helping the learner to not only understand who the disinherited are, but also recognize the world's desire for humanity to be awakened.
>
> Howard Thurman's book is significant for spiritual formation. Thurman examines Jesus' teachings that point to the inward spirit that enables them to have a heart for those who are marginalized, disenfranchised, oppressed and excluded. It is this spirit that is evidenced in the people who confront the circumstances that leaves people in their communities *disinherited*, deprived of the right to pursue a fulfilling life.

Political Formation

The spiritual formation at First Corinthian Baptist also incorporates the teaching of politics. Through study of *The Politics of Jesus* by Obery Hendricks, the course looks to "explore Jesus' strategic models of engaging sociopolitical contradictions that are plaguing our nation. How is it possible to profess a belief in Jesus, yet ignore the suffering of the poor and needy? In light of heated political debates, *The Politics of Jesus* will implore the learner to observe the life and mind of Jesus of Nazareth through this provocative critique of modern politicians 'of faith.'"[8]

This is a very critical book and course for a church to offer. Political formation is not something I have observed being aggressively addressed in a church. We often hear sermons and may from time to time encourage responsibilities during elections. I see this course included as a part of spiritual formation having taken the role of Christians in political action a step further.

Gender Awareness

The courses on gender awareness are included, I think, as a matter of justice. Melissa Harris-Perry's *Sister Citizen* provides content to "ignite a long-overdue conversation about black women's political identity formation. Harris-Perry moves from locating shame as a tool of social control, to the empowering stories of the black women in American History. *Sister Citizen* locates black women's political identity at the center of all political thought." Melissa Harris-Perry, a professor and political commentator, is a leading voice on examining national political and social affairs. Her book *Sister Citizen* places emphasis on the role of women of color in impacting and leading change as a part of their political and personal identity. Christians need to be competent and engaged politically as we work to bring about a more just society.

Spirituality

Students in another course are studying *Holy Play,* a book by Kirk Byron Jones, which the FCBC catalog says "challenges us to take an adventurous path with God to unleash your purpose. Purpose is an open invitation from God to playfully (joyfully and creatively) imagine and live your boldest dreams."

Another course in the church's catalog is using the well-known book by Richard Foster, *The Celebration of Disciplines.* The catalog copy reads: "Discover a richer spiritual life infused with joy, peace, and a deeper understanding of God through the 'classic Disciplines,' or central spiritual practices, of the Christian faith. Learners will be compelled to embark on a journey of prayer and spiritual growth."

Ministerial Leader Formation

Also offered are courses specifically for current and past seminarians related to preaching. One that stands out the most as relating to the focus of this writing is *The Spiritual Visionary and the Cultural Architect.* First Corinthian goes one step further in providing for the development of future generations. They have developed a center that focuses on "birthing valiant visionaries."[9]

The Dream Center is a multifaceted transformative hub that "unearths unlimited possibilities, while simultaneously shaping the winds of perception . . . by way of both unparalleled and unmatched programming."[10] The center focuses on leadership development, economic empowerment, and creative arts as a part of their spiritual formation of all generations.

MODEL FOR COLLECTIVE ACTIVISM
Housing Ministries of American Baptists in Wisconsin

When you arrive at the website of Housing Ministries of American Baptists in Wisconsin, (www.hmabw.org) you see this statement: "A Ministry of Hope and Opportunity." The ministry's name would lead you to believe that it is simply about housing, but it is much more. Housing is a provision for those who otherwise would be challenged to acquire a safe and sanitary place to reside, and that alone would be a valuable work. But the vision and call of this ministry go much further. Housing Ministries's mission is to provide affordable housing and services to individuals who qualify for residency in their developments.

Housing Ministries is a ministry to six low-income communities managed by a unique approach to housing as described in their mission statement. This unique method incorporates and assists adults in empowering themselves to improve their circumstances and achieve productive, fruitful, and healthy life choices for themselves and their children. Rev. Dr. Carmen Porco, executive director, explains that he and the board, consisting of local church members, are committed to "change the face of poverty in America by changing the perceptions about people who experience economic poverty." The leadership does this not just to be socially correct, but to be theologically just and prophetically responsive. (The quotes in this section are from a personal interview held on October 12, 2013.)

Reverend Porco says, "We need to view [the residents] as capable persons who could provide for the community if they had the same level of resources that others enjoy." Encouraging collective action, he says, "We also need to realize that working on an individual basis alone is not going to resolve the systemic problems. We need to develop not only a systems approach, we need to develop a systemic approach that provides the sequential levels of service that meet the various growth cycle needs that we all go through. In this instance we need to recognize that it is not only individuals in communities of poverty that are disenfranchised, it is also the institutions in communities of poverty that are disenfranchised as well."

Reverend Porco's prophetic leadership is informed by sociological, political, and relational underpinnings. About this, Porco says, "We are required by faith to build on the strength of our common humanity and not segregate ourselves according to social order. A social order built on distinctions of difference based on race, ethnicity, gender, economic status, educational status, and other constructs that tear the quilt of community diminishes both those who create these artificial distinctions and those who are set off as different."

He further reflects on the revolutionary work of Christ, saying, "What a revolutionarily different perspective when we look at the distinctions Christ made! Christ asks us to redefine 'neighbor' according to standards of compassion and need, not proximity and similarity. Christ defines himself not with those of similar heritage and social standing, but with the hungry, the thirsty, the sick, the prisoners. We must ask ourselves, 'How are we to engage one another in the limited time we are given to journey through this time and space? How do we make meaningful contributions to realizing God's kingdom, as well as by the recipients of grace extended to us by others?'"

For Housing Ministries, housing is not merely a physical issue. It is an issue of acceptance, interdependence, belonging, and human rights. This philosophy informs and shapes their approach to management, staffing, programming, and collaborations. The philosophy of organizational development is to integrate human services into the structure of housing management. The program philosophy, rich in social gospel theological principles, is multidisciplinary. Psychology, sociology, business, ethics, organizational development, and social justice practices are at the center of the programs.

A Unique Management Method

Housing Ministries' approach is unique. They integrate property management and a human service organization into community management by developing a systems approach rather than using the old strategy of doing for individuals who are experiencing economic poverty. They develop the internal potential and asset of the community by hiring residents first for all jobs. They developed a program depth that is focused on education and employment training for all ages. The program is designed to meet the various stages of human growth and development that occur in the life cycle. But this ministry is not insular and for the internal community only. A part of their vision is to also build the internal capacity to have a meaningful impact on the external community through strategic alliances.

The board of directors consists of pastors, laypeople, community advocates, and persons in higher education. The valuable partnerships go beyond church bodies, for the ministry shares its mission with two universities, one seminary, and early childhood program providers. This collective action engages the leadership of the persons who reside in these six communities to determine their own paths through employment within the housing communities.

Vital Collaborations

Housing Ministries collaborates in ministry with national, regional, and local church mission. Historically, the American Baptist Churches USA through the American Baptist Home Mission Societies, the American Baptist Churches of Wisconsin, and the Housing Ministries of American Baptists in Wisconsin have worked together for more than thirty years under visionary and prophetic leadership that has guided this ministry of transformation and advocacy for the economically poor in Milwaukee and Madison. This model of ministry, however, has been reviewed and replicated in other places in the United States and in other countries.

The collective action goes even further. These communities are federally funded through Section 8 of the Department of Housing and Urban Development (HUD). Housing Ministries of American Baptists in Wisconsin is a successful model of a mission serving for the good of the economically poor. Church, academy, and government are sharing in a common cause by working together. Other providers meet the day care, Head Start, after-school, adult education, and employment training needs of the residents. These programs promote the self-sufficiency and independence of their low-income target population. In 1997, Rev. Porco received four National Partnership for Reinventing Government's Hammer Awards from then Vice President Al Gore for his work in developing the learning centers. These awards were a result of Rev. Porco's work in helping to start the Neighborhood networks concept within HUD. Later, in 2005, Carmen was awarded the first Champion of Change award from HUD, which is now an award being handled by the White House. These awards recognize the total perspective of what this model of ministry has done in transforming a systems approach to housing and a model of an integrative delivery system of services to enhance community.

The perspective of a systems approach and an integrative delivery system of services makes the resident leadership in management an even more unique aspect about this ministry model. The employees and the management are residents, some having lived in these communities for thirty years. This residential approach is the ministry plan that helps the poor to empower themselves by managing and further developing the programs that are at work here.

Head Start and child care services, adult college programs on site, urban leadership development, computer training, and award-winning video recording and filmmaking are the major programs and services that are offered and supported by the Housing Ministries. Each property is unique through the programs offered.

Family Programs
The family housing properties offer large neighborhood learning centers that extend learning to the entire family. In long-standing partnerships with colleges and universities, these learning centers have helped to meet community needs and eradicate poverty among housing residents and the most immediate community.

Adult Education
College degree offerings are made available to the residents and surrounding community to help the participants achieve a college education to equip them for their work and help them tap into other interests with a degree in hand. These courses are offered onsite at the learning center. Students have graduated and gone on to receive higher degrees.

Residents are also provided scholarship support to attend school to complete their education at a school of their choice. The modest scholarships provide extraordinary support for adults who ordinarily would be on their own. This is one way Housing Ministries is more than housing; it is transformation.

The Urban Leadership Internship Program helps individuals who are seeking to serve God in community, whether in the traditional parish model or in advocacy/social justice models. Internships provide students from universities and seminaries who are studying the social, political, and cultural dynamics of transformation within "communities of poverty" to understand how to become change agents and partners with persons in poverty. The internship goals are to create potential for leadership development in the area of housing ministry, to promote this type of ministry and service in the academic world, and to provide their residents and the people they serve with the opportunity of serving, as well as being served, by the interns.

The interns receive tangible hands-on exposure to community management contexts and learn the principles of being a housing manager and service provider. They also develop pastoral skills in community.

Early Childhood Education

Great care is given to the education and development of children at Housing Ministries. Day care services assist parents in making sure their children are properly cared for, provided with learning opportunities, and involved in community. The Head Start program offers children a continuum of learning. Summer and after-school enrichment programs are also available so that the children and families are given every advantage possible to achieve their goals.

Models of Ministries Bring Vital Spirit, Vital Service

Legacy leaders, parish engagement, servant leadership, spiritual formation, and collective activism—these models provide a panoramic view of the vast variety of ministries that are engaging people in service that is significant for their lives. The financial resources for each ministry model vary, but each is committed to be faithful to what God has strategically located them to do among those who need their presence the most.

> They gave offerings of whatever they could—far more than they could afford!—pleading for the privilege of helping out in the relief of poor Christians. This was totally spontaneous, entirely their own idea, and caught us completely off guard. What explains it was that they had first given themselves unreservedly to God and to us. The other giving simply flowed out of the purposes of God working in their lives. (2 Corinthians 8:3-5, MSG)

Notes

1. This information was taken from the All Saints Catholic Church Member Covenant that was provided during the interview.

2. The quotes in this paragraph were taken from a video on www.allsaintsmilwaukee.org. All other quotes were from a personal interview with the author.

3. Michelle Boorstein, "Activist D.C. Church Embraces Transition in Name of Its Mission," *Washington Post*, January 6, 2009, http://www.washingtonpost.com/wp-dyn/content/article/2009/01/05/AR2009010503341.html.

4. Information from website of First Corinthian Baptist Church, New York City, 2013, www.fcbcnyc.org/about-us-mission.

5. Erwin Raphael McManus, *The Barbarian Way: Unleash the Untamed Faith Within* (Thomas Nelson: Nashville, 2005), 6.

6. Ibid, 5.

7. Howard Thurman, *Jesus and the Disinherited* (Boston: Beacon Press, 1976).

8. Quote is taken from the course description provided in the First Corinthian Baptist Church of New York's 2013 Spiritual Formation Course Book.

9. Ibid., The Dream Center.

10. Ibid.

CHAPTER 9

Putting the Principles into Action

> Service and activism represent flip sides of a two-sided
> coin called Christian discipleship.
>
> —Adam Taylor[1]

"But you will receive power when the Holy Spirit comes on you; and you will be my witnesses in Jerusalem, and in all Judea and Samaria, and to the ends of the earth" (Acts 1:8). This great commission is also a great promise. Jesus promises us the Holy Spirit, our strongest supporter and resource for living as witnesses in our church, in our surroundings, in our families, in institutions, in our community and country, and in the farthest reaches of our world.

"But you will receive power when the Holy Spirit comes on you." It is in Christ through the *power* of the Holy Spirit that we are able to accomplish all that God has for us to be and to do. Without the Holy Spirit we can do nothing. With the Holy Spirit all things are possible; all things are secured. God gives us great confidence that, as the saying goes, "God will not lead you where God cannot keep you." The ministry models chapter 8 all have one common resource—the power of the Holy Spirit.

Lessons Learned

So now we will look at what we have learned from these ministry models. What principles undergird their work? Perhaps not present in every model but certainly indicated across these models are some guiding truths that can be applied in church settings, in our individual lives, and in our work and spheres of significance. In thinking about your own context and its realities, you may perceive the path ahead to be somewhat daunting, but be encouraged. There is a Helper—a Provider and Power given to us so that we can be witnesses in our Jerusalem, our Judea, and to the ends of the earth, wherever that place may be.

As we review these model ministries, we find that the commonalities, diverse and unique approaches, and ministry philosophies are rich. Principles emerge that may become foundational understandings and practices for any ministry that fulfills its call to equip, empower, and "ordain" people to make the connections between their Christian spirituality and their capacity to touch God's creation in a personal way. It is possible that by adhering to a set of governing principles, any local church can build, redirect, or reinforce its current ministry strategies.

Of course, as was discussed in chapter 6, mission and ministry are practiced within a specific context, culture, and community that have particularities that must be understood and leveraged for the developed ministry to be effective. Also, as shared in chapter 3, all of us are called to be engaged in our spheres of significance where we extend our calling as Christians to be present, whether that presence is in our families, with our neighbors, at our workplaces, in community institutions, or in global environments. Preparing disciples for this kind of living is the work of the church: "Christ himself gave the apostles, the prophets, the evangelists, the pastors and teachers, to equip his people for works of service, so that the body of Christ may be built up" (Ephesians 4:11-12).

Seven principles have emerged from my research of the models discussed in this book. These principles of formation and transformation ministries have been identified from three sources: (1) research and interviews with ministry models, (2) observation of practice, and (3) Scripture, with Scripture being the strongest source for the principles in faith and practice.

From these principles you should be able to extract and identify, particularize, and individualize the insights and strategies that are applicable for your church context. The result is that your church can better prepare members to serve God in transformative work and service, fulfilling God's purpose, which has been the purposes of their own lives.

Seven Formative Principles

1. *The Leadership Principle.* Leadership's vocation and calling must be in alignment with the church's ministry, mission, and purpose in order to further the church's spiritual legacy (Joshua 1:1-17).

2. *The Word Principle.* Preaching and teaching are at the center of God's plan for a relevant, relational, and rejuvenating ministry (2 Timothy 3:16-17).

3. *The Formation Principle.* Spiritual formation is critical in a disciple-making ministry that empowers and engages persons in their surroundings (2 Timothy 1:6-14).

4. *The Communal Principle.* Prayer, worship, and fellowship in community sustain an active and engaged ministry as a spiritual discipline (Acts 2:42-47; Hebrews 10:24-25).

5. *The Service Principle.* Faithful discipleship is service as mission done individually and collectively (Luke 22:24-27). "Service and activism represent flip sides of a two-sided coin called Christian discipleship."[2]

6. *The Partnership Principle.* Commitment to ministry partnerships through collaboration and collective action expands our capacity for effectiveness (Luke 5:1-11).

7. *The Stewardship Principle.* The stewardship of resources enables our reach, anchors our ministry, and demonstrates our faithfulness (1 Peter 4:8-11).

Practicing the Principles

The work of the pastor and other church leaders in putting these seven principles into practice is a formative ministry for preparing others to serve. Pastors in particular are in the place of helping their parishioners discern God's plan for their lives.

Identify Called Leadership—The Leadership Principle

Leadership's vocation and calling must be in strong alignment with the church's ministry, mission, and purpose to preserve and advance a spiritual legacy (based on Joshua 1:1-17).

Clergy and lay leaders alike have a vital role in making disciples and serving in church ministries. Pastoral leadership is the office through which God has chosen to "shepherd the flock," communicate ministry vision, and bear primary responsibility for the church's spiritual growth. Marvin McMickle says that "many churches make decisions about what they expect from their pastor without seeking from their pool of candidates or the person presently serving in that position anything that approaches 'a conception or overarching vision' that would inform them in the exercise of their duties."[3] McMickle further cites from Thomas C. Oden's *Pastoral Theology*, "The importance of the office of pastor still quietly pleads with us to think with extraordinary care about the better and worse ways in which that office might be conceived and practiced."[4]

The story of the prophet Moses and his successor, Joshua, gives us a very solid indication of the importance of leadership and proper leadership transition, keeping up the momentum of the ministry begun by prior leadership. Moses' prophetic ministry was closely observed by his assistant Joshua.

When time had come for the end of Moses' ministry (through his death, but a transition nonetheless), the Lord charged Joshua, saying, "Moses my servant is dead. Now then, you and all these people, get ready to cross the Jordan River into the land I am about to give to them" (Joshua 1:2). Joshua accepted the call of God to take the people forward into the Promised Land as God had begun through Moses. What God begins in a ministry with one leader may be continued through his or her successor. This is what we see here in the case of Moses and Joshua and also in the ministry model of Calvary Baptist Church (see pages 100–104).

Both the local church and the new or existing pastor need to have a deep sense of the mission and ministry call and charism that God has placed on the church and within the minister. This alignment makes for a very vital ministry when a church is serving its community in prophetic works as God has led and continues to call them forward until the vision is fulfilled or God changes the call. The congregation corporately works out their ministry by the leading of the Holy Spirit as their collective witness in the community.

But members also have a call to fulfill God's purposes for themselves as individuals through their own services rendered in the places God has placed them—in their families, neighborhoods, workplaces, civic organizations, or other places in the world. Paul, in his letter to the Romans, encouraged believers, writing, "Don't copy the behavior and customs of this world, but let God transform you into a new person by changing the way you think. Then you will learn to know God's will for you, which is good and pleasing and perfect" (Romans 12:2, NLT). Paul continued to teach them about the motivational gift that God had given them in order that they might better discover their particular role in the church and world:

> In his grace, God has given us different gifts for doing certain things well. So if God has given you the ability to prophesy, speak out with as much faith as God has given you. If your gift is serving others, serve them well. If you are a teacher, teach well. If your gift is to encourage others, be encouraging. If it is giving, give generously. If God has given you leadership ability, take the responsibility seriously. And if you have a gift for showing kindness to others, do it gladly. (Romans 12:6-8, NLT)

Obey your urge—that is what I get from the Romans 12 text. Obey your urge and follow your nudge. God places in each of us the urge to do something. This urge grows up inside of us as we are being renewed and transformed for God's good work. This internal stirring gets us moving in the direction God wants us to go. As we go we become connected to God's purpose in the strongest kind of way, and we feel alive, authentic, and aligned. This is where God wants us to be.

Joshua was right where God wanted him to be: with the people of Israel, leading them across the Jordan River to press their way into the land God had promised them. No matter how difficult and challenging the task, God wanted him in that leadership post. God, knowing the work Joshua was going to embrace, instilled in Joshua all the confidence he would need. He said:

> I promise you what I promised Moses: "Wherever you set foot, you will be on land I have given you. . . . No one will be able to stand against you as long as you live. For I will be with you as I was with Moses. I will not fail you or abandon you. Be strong and courageous, for you are the one who will lead these people to possess all the land I swore to their ancestors I would give them. Be strong and very courageous. Be careful to obey all the instructions Moses gave you. Do not deviate from them, turning either to the right or to the left. Then you will be successful in everything you do. Study this Book of Instruction continually. Meditate on it day and night so you will be sure to obey everything written in it. Only then will you prosper and succeed in all you do. This is my command—be strong and courageous! Do not be afraid or discouraged. For the LORD your God is with you wherever you go." (Joshua 1:3, 5-9, NLT)

"Be strong and courageous! Do not be afraid or discouraged. For the LORD your God is with you wherever you go." How often are church people asked by God to take leadership of something and they have doubt or even fear about the task? It is probably somewhat of a common occurrence, or at least expected, for God hastily adds the instruction for Joshua not to be afraid. Whether you are clergy or laity, God says to be strong and courageous, not to be afraid; and, no matter what, do not be discouraged. It behooves us to remember that God is with us wherever we go. Your calling and vocation must be in strong alignment with the church's ministry, mission, and purpose to preserve and advance a spiritual legacy of transforming your community for Christ.

The Bible Equips Good Works—The Word Principle
Preaching and teaching are at the center of God's plan for a relevant, relational, and rejuvenating ministry (based on 2 Timothy 3:16-17).

> All scripture is God-breathed and is useful for teaching, rebuking, correcting and training in righteousness, so that the servant of God may be thoroughly equipped for every good work. (2 Timothy 3:16-17)

From the ministry models we looked at in chapter 8, we can glean three areas of common ministry methods: the central place of Scripture throughout the ministries, the prevalence of prominent prophetic preaching, and accessible discipleship ministries and Bible studies. These approaches bring strength to ministries.

The Central Place of Scripture throughout the Ministries / The central place of the Scriptures in the lives of Jesus' disciples cannot be overstated. The psalmist wrote, "Your word is a lamp for my feet, a light on my path" (Psalm 119:105). And "But their delight is in the law of the Lord, and on his law they meditate day and night" (Psalm 1:2 NRSV). Another verse says, "The word of God is alive and active. Sharper than any double-edged sword, it penetrates even to dividing soul and spirit, joints and marrow" (Hebrews 4:12). And as we read in 2 Timothy 3:16-17, the Bible is useful for teaching, rebuking, correcting, and training so that as servants of God we may be thoroughly equipped for every good work.

The pastors featured in the ministry models unanimously identified preaching and teaching ministries as foremost in their ministry approach. While preaching is primary, the foci of the preached messages, of course, do vary. The main purpose of preaching is to spread the gospel so that people might hear it and be saved. Preaching of Scripture is also for the spiritual growth of the church. It motivates us to fulfill God's purposes in our lives and in the world. Although Scripture is the main source for preaching and teaching, the ministry models shared in common the incorporation of other writings and resources to enhance their discipleship training and Bible studies. I will discuss this in a section below.

Prominent Prophetic Preaching / In reviewing the ministry models, I observed that the ministers strike a very intentional balance of preached messages. Gospel preachers' messages are for seekers who have an inquiring spirit toward the things of God, but they are also for disciples who desire to grow deeper in their Christian walk.

Preaching, and teaching, is a concentration in the church's own ministry that leverages a preached word that is prophetic and provocative. This kind of preaching advances a social gospel, a liberating gospel, that motivates and calls for the pursuit of righteousness and justice. The role of the believer in service to others is to transform and bring change in their communities, in public policy, and in corporate systems. This preaching may draw heavily from the prophetic books of the Old Testament, namely Isaiah, Micah, Hosea, Amos, and Nehemiah. Also prominent in such preaching is liberation theology, primarily drawn from the books of Exodus and Joshua—preaching that relates the account of Israel's deliverance from slavery in Egypt to that of God's will for all oppressed peoples through acts of social justice and social change, a biblical justice.

Accessible Discipleship Ministries and Bible Study / *Christianity Today*, in a 2010 article titled "Why Johnny Can't Read the Bible," reported on a Barna Group survey that asked American Christians to rate their spiritual maturity based on activities such as worship, service, and evangelism. Christians offered the harshest self-evaluation of their Bible knowledge, with 25 percent calling themselves "not too mature" or "not at all mature."[5] For our model ministries, Bible study is a core ministry that is delivered in a variety of methods so that their congregations can increase their knowledge and application of the Bible in their daily lives and service.

Because people have diverse schedules and sometimes long distances to travel, churches offer multiple opportunities for Bible study and teaching to provide better access to learning and training opportunities. Some ways of doing this follow:

Multiple Bible study sections. While offering more than one section of a Bible study may be a challenge, doing so builds on the relational aspect of a ministry. It acknowledges the needs of the participants by offering them choices that better fit their personal and family schedules. For example, some churches offer Bible studies early in the morning, late afternoon and/or evening sessions. Others may offer sessions on multiple days; for example, a Sunday afternoon session, a midweek session, and a Friday night or Saturday morning opportunity. Paired with these learning opportunities is the option to participate virtually for those with distance and travel limitations.

Podcasts, live streaming, other technologies. Not new but worthy of mentioning here are the ways that technology is being leveraged by the church to give access to the congregants and others who may want to participate in Christian education. Even other faith-based sources that have online learning are useful. While online sites need to be vetted for their consistency with Christian teaching and doctrine, they can be a substantial help in expanding a church's capacity to teach and train laypeople. Researching these organizations on the Web is not difficult, and partnership with them can be a very substantial collaboration.

Paul wrote to Timothy, "You then, my son, be strong in the grace that is in Christ Jesus. And the things you have heard me say in the presence of many witnesses entrust to reliable people who will also be qualified to teach others" (2 Timothy 2:1-2). It is the church's responsibility to "entrust to reliable people" the Word of God so they will be "qualified to teach others" not only through words but through deeds. Disciples generate disciples (see Matthew 28:18-20). The next section on the formation principle discusses this further.

Be Intentional about Disciple Making and Spiritual Formation— The Formation Principle

Spiritual formation is that ministry that leads us into mature witness and service (based on 2 Timothy 1:6-14).

What may be traditionally called Christian education or discipleship training at one church may be called spiritual formation at another. The general aim of these ministries is the same however they may be labeled. Education and formation ministries seek to foster growth in church members, leaders, and all who participate in such ministries. Spiritual formation may better capture the lifelong intent of a comprehensive all-around engagement in matters of faith, spiritual growth, discernment, calling, service, and Christian lifestyle. Formation is intentional, direct, communal, personal, and diverse. The premise is that individuals and communities such as a church can be shaped for a life of service.

Second Timothy 1:6-14 helps us understand the essence of formation. Paul wrote to Timothy as a spiritual father would. He gave Timothy guidance on how to nurture and nourish his faith and his gifts, which were first placed in Timothy by God, then nurtured by Timothy's grandmother and mother, and finally encouraged and mentored by Paul. As Timothy matured, it was his Christian responsibility to "stir up the gifts" that were within him. That stirring into flame is our work in cooperation with the Holy Spirit's continual shaping of us through our experiences and learning.

Our experiences stir up in us a passion that brings to our awareness the places in the world that touch our hearts and beg for our involvement. They stir up anger within us about injustices and issues that violate God's purposes in the world. And our experiences and circumstances stir up a realization of the greatest gift God calls forth in us–love.

Our everyday realities and the things we go through from our childhood through our adulthood are formative. My own experiences growing up during the civil rights movement and personal experiences of discrimination, segregation, racial inequality, economic disparities, riots, and police brutality have formed my sense of moral responsibility for social justice, equality, and economic justice. My experience with my home church being engaged in the progress for civil rights in my hometown shaped how I understand the role of the church in moral agency and as witnesses working to bring social justice through spiritual activism.

"For this reason," Paul told Timothy, "I remind you to fan into flame the gift of God, which is in you through the laying on of my hands. For the Spirit God gave us does not make us timid, but gives us power, love and self-discipline" (2 Timothy 1:6-7).

Focus on Developing and Growing Community—The Communal Principle
Prayer, worship, and fellowship in community sustain spiritual discipline and growth (based on Acts 2:42-47 and Hebrews 10:24-25).

Community was discussed in chapter 6 as being a structural design that God intended from the very beginning and throughout God's interaction in the biblical story. The ministry models support this principle in their practices, and the first-century church was grounded in communal gatherings and commitments from its inception. Acts 2 shows the Jerusalem church's commitment to fellowship: "They devoted themselves to the apostles' teaching and to fellowship, to the breaking of bread and to prayer" (v. 42). That kind of devotion is what makes *teaching and learning, fellowship, breaking of bread*, and *prayer* the pillars that build, grow, and unify community. The Jerusalem church gives us these four pillars of communal life.

The tone of this Acts text seems to be directly referencing the behaviors and character of the Jerusalem church. "They devoted themselves" refers to the nature of the believers' involvement or participation. They were present out of their devotion to God, to the community, and to their own spiritual growth. *Proskartereō eimi*, translated here as "devoted to," means to be steadfast and unrelenting. This is the driving principle of building and maintaining what it means to be communal.

Four Pillars of Communal Life / *Teaching and learning.* Earlier I discussed the church's role in offering Bible study, discipleship training, and spiritual formation opportunities. Here I want to turn to the believers' role in maintaining their commitment to Bible study and other learning opportunities. The early believers were consistent in their participation in learning. They learned from the apostles, and then they learned by doing. They were sent out to serve in Jerusalem, Judea, Samaria, and the uttermost parts of the world.

Three very effective hands-on learning methods are service learning, experiential learning, and service immersion. These methods are especially popular with high school and college-age students, and they are now becoming more appealing to adults, particularly retirees. While learners are serving others, they are also completing a course of study.

Fellowship. Koinonia, meaning "fellowship, community, communion," expresses a common bond and intimacy experienced through sharing. As helpful as our virtual means of staying connected is in our mobile and dispersed culture, being in the presence of one another is still the greatest way of relating, finding relevance, and being rejuvenated. A sense of belonging is vital. Our significance is affirmed and validated in our fellowships, in our sharing of a common good, whether that takes place in our homes among our families, in our neighborhoods among friends, or in our churches, workplaces, or organizations.

Breaking of bread. "Breaking of bread" in the Bible is a reference to the early church sharing meals together as a common practice, or discipline. Sharing meals as a spiritual discipline brought a grace that strengthened their fellowship. But breaking of bread goes well beyond that. It can be experienced outside the church in a variety of settings where people gather regularly. The following example shows how one faith-based organization made their fellowship come alive to this Acts 2 text during a staff retreat. I share it below in its entirety with permission from the developer, Rev. Dr. Ronald Carlson, who serves as missional church strategist with the American Baptist Home Mission Societies of the American Baptist Churches USA.

AN INVITATION TO WORSHIP:

Throughout the history of God's people eating together, "the breaking of bread" has been a hallmark of worship and community formation.

An ancient Israel and Judaism yet today cele-brates the Passover, breaking bread as a reminder of God's actions of deliverance, past, present, and future, as a reminder of Israel's com-mon identity as God's people.

The early followers of Jesus and Christ-follow-ers yet today celebrate the Lord's Supper, break-ing bread as a perpetual reminder of the cruci-fied and resurrected Christ's forgiving presence, giving common identity to the diverse people of God who comprise the church.

The breaking of bread, for God's people, has also served and continues to serve as a primary means of inclusive hospitality. Family, strangers, aliens, sojourners, clean and unclean, saints and sinners and even heavenly-guests, have all been invited by God's people to break bread together, to "come and dine."

In this, our closing worship service of staff week, we all are invited to break bread together literally and figuratively as we gather around these tables of fellowship celebrating being a community of faith on mission with God with its simple table that is set before us with breads, refreshing fruit, and beverage. We are all invited to it as guests and hosts seeking to find and to provide community in an alienated world.

Hospitality, the simple act of breaking bread together, is neither sacrament nor ordinance and yet perhaps it is both in a more inclusive way. For it was Jesus himself who reminded his people: "Where two or more are gathered together in my name, there I am in the midst of them."

In keeping with our theme, Celebrating Being a Community of Faith that Creates Community, we invite you to sit at these tables, break bread together, and celebrate God's presence and our presence with one another as a community.

In keeping tradition with the historic practices of breaking bread together, we are going to reflect on our past, our present, and our hope for the future. Three sets of questions will help guide our table-conversations. We will spend about 15 minutes in conversation around each question before concluding each segment of sharing with a hymn or song.

REFLECTING ON THE PAST:

Beginning to break bread together, we reflect on our past.

Question 1: What role did eating with others play in your upbringing and in shaping your personal identity?

Question Hint: What favorite table experience, foods, or common meal do you remember from your childhood and adolescence?

Text: Acts 2:42 (read by one of the leaders after 15 minutes of discussion)

Song: "Let us Break Bread Together"
REFLECTING ON OUR TIMES TOGETHER:
Continuing to break bread together, we consider our present times as an _____ community.

Question 2: How has eating together enhanced the building of community among staff?

Or, consider these questions: What other-than-eating experience(s) stand out in your mind as helpful in building relationships with other staff members? What experiences have contributed to your sense of belonging to the _____ community?

Text: Acts 2:42 (read again after 15 minutes)
Song: "Bond of Love"
LOOKING TOWARD GOD'S FUTURE:
As we look toward God's future, we recognize that not only are we invited to participate in the _____ community, but also we are called to be agents who create and foster community outside of _____—wherever God sends us.

Question 3: What behaviors tend to build a sense of community outside of the _____ circle?

Or, consider these questions: What experience(s) stand out in your mind in which you were a part of a community outside of _____? In what community-building action outside of _____? In what community-building action outside of _____ are you willing to engage in the coming year?

Text: Acts 2:42 (read again after 15 minutes)
Song: "We Are One in the Spirit"
Closing Prayer: Recite the Lord's Prayer together followed by a moment of silence in

which we each pray for the person on our right
and on our left.

Fellowship can be experienced in our spheres of significance when
we approach them as places of hospitality where we are guests and/or
hosts, either being welcomed or inviting. The breaking of bread is literal yet simple. It is sitting and supping one with another but not to be
concerned whether the meal is sufficient. It is the welcoming and inviting and being present, being with another, that is of most significance.

Prayer. Such presence and being with others is not just a prelude to
prayer; it is prayer. It is listening and caring, talking and sharing, holding
and lifting each other as gift and grace. At All Saints Catholic Church,
Father Carl includes remembrance of all members of the parish in
prayer as a covenantal practice. Pastor Walton at Calvary Baptist
Church provides opportunities for communal prayer on Wednesday
evenings and also on Saturday mornings. The reality is that prayer is
communal in and of itself. God invites us to the communal gathering of
our spirit with God's Spirit: "God is spirit, and his worshipers must worship in the Spirit and in truth" (John 4:24). "We do not know what we
ought to pray for, but the Spirit himself intercedes for us through word-
less groans" (Romans 8:26). Prayer is one way of our relating to God
and relating with one another.

It is no wonder that the Jerusalem church held prayer as one of its pillars of communal life. After all, it is God who calls us to be with others
and together to be with God. My intent here is not to give a prescription
for prayer, a set of prayer styles, or an array of prayer programs. Rather,
I intend to bring out the central role of prayer as creating the complete
triangle of the community gathered and dispersed. Prayer brings us into
communion with God through the Holy Spirit. The catalyst that ener-
gizes the interaction of you, others, and God is the Holy Spirit. The
Holy Spirit also communicates our moans and groans to God as stated
in Acts 8:26: "Likewise the Spirit helps us in our weakness; for we do
not know how to pray as we ought, but that very Spirit intercedes with

sighs too deep for words. And God, who searches the heart, knows what is the mind of the Spirit, because the Spirit intercedes for the saints according to the will of God" (NRSV).

The figure below depicts the interaction that is created when we join together in prayer.

Figure 9.1

Keep Service Primary; Encourage and Support Personal Mission— The Service Principle

Faithful discipleship is service done individually and collectively (based on Luke 22:24-27).

Faithful discipleship begins with our taking on Christ's likeness in every way. A key way to imitate Christ is to serve others with Christlike humility, a humility like that demonstrated by Jesus when he washed his disciples' feet at the last supper. When Jesus heard the bickering that was beginning among his disciples about who was going to be the greatest, he chided them, saying, "Kings like to throw their weight around and people in authority like to give themselves fancy titles. It's not going to be that way with you. Let the senior among you become like the junior; let the leader act the part of the servant" (Luke 22:24-26, MSG).

Jesus taught servant leadership through this exchange. Just to make it clear, he then asked his disciples who was greater, the one who sat at the table or the one who served. He told them the greater was the one who sat at the table, yet he came as one who served. This model set by Jesus is our prime example of servant leadership for faith and practice. In John's Gospel Jesus does one more gesture: he provides the prime example of a servant leader to follow as a way of life. He gets up from the table and, removing his robe and putting it around himself as an apron, washes his disciples' feet.

Develop Relationships with True Partners, Collaborators, and Sponsors—The Partnership Principle

Commitment to ministry partnerships, collaboration and collective action, expands capacity for effectiveness. Inclusion is a priority (based on Luke 5:1-11).

Each of the model ministries discussed in this book said that their efforts depend on the partnerships and collaborations they develop. American Baptists have lived with a conviction that we can do more together than we can do apart. I recently heard the impressive saying "I can't. You can't. But we can."

This partner principle was at play when Jesus told his disciples to get back into their fishing boats, push out into the deep, and cast their nets. "It was no sooner said than done—a huge haul of fish, straining the nets past capacity. They waved to their partners in the other boat to come help them. They filled both boats, nearly swamping them with the catch" (Luke 5:6-7, MSG). Partnership is a biblical principle. When our own capacity is tested and we find that we need help, getting help from other like-purposed people, organizations, churches, or institutions is wisdom.

So, what makes for true partnership? I have used various kinds of partnerships in my different capacities. Sometimes we refer to someone as a partner who is really serving as a collaborator. I have discovered that true partnership can be different from a collaboration. Both are useful, and both are needed in doing transformation ministry. I recognize a *true* partner in this way: a person, group, organization, or institution who *joins/unites with another in a shared exploration, development, and advancement of a goal and who will commit economic support or share the work in the endeavor or initiative.*

A collaborator, on the other hand, is a person, group, church, organization, or institution who *shares in the development and mission, combining their efforts with yours on a specific and identified initiative, event, program, or process in ways that support and provide participant pools and/or services.*

An influencer is a person, group, organization, church, or institution who *provides their name, networks, connections, expertise, rapport, reputation, business, ministry, leadership, or other virtues to bring value that will advance to targeted and identified groups and demographic and geographic areas, the exploration, development, and mission of your group or church.*

Just for further distinction, I refer to a participant as a person, group, church, organization, or institution who *takes part in a specific event, initiative, training, or process for the purpose of gaining education, resources, and connections to support their work, discipleship, and mission.*

With these distinctions, we are able to share our mission and work with others in appropriate ways that meet the interest, resources, purposes, and calling of those involved. Partners, collaborators, influencers, and participants make it possible for us to do more together than we are able to do apart. This makes for greater inclusion, which is a priority. The disciples were able to increase their capacity by being inclusive. They waved for partners in the other boat. Those partners brought their resource, their boat. Not only is this good partnership, but it is also good stewardship.

Be Entrepreneurial by Leveraging Available Resources to Support Ministries—The Stewardship Principle

The stewardship of resources enables our reach, anchors our ministry, and demonstrates our faithfulness (based on 1 Peter 4:8-11).

Above all, love each other deeply, because love covers over a multitude of sins. Offer hospitality to one another without grumbling. Each of you should use whatever gift you have received to serve others, as faithful stewards of God's grace in its various forms. If anyone speaks, they should do so as one who speaks the very words of God. If anyone serves, they should do so with the strength God provides, so that in all things God may be praised through Jesus Christ. To him be the glory and the power forever and ever. Amen. (1 Peter 4:8-11)

A central operating principle in organizational life is to make the choice to function in an entrepreneurial fashion. Being entrepreneurial is more than just financial. It is how we leverage, access, and use all resources for the glory of God.

According to 1 Peter 4:8-11, resources include people—human resources. Our capacity to love and our spiritual and natural gifts are used to serve others. Our homes, centers, and churches are physical resources we have available to support the ministries and our service to others.

The entrepreneurial spirit that is prominent today was present in Peter's counsel to the early Christian church. This text was written during a time when the church was scattering into areas where they would have no support, no safe place to stay, no food—nothing. If the Christians who had resources did not share them as faithful stewards, these persons would have suffered by going without, and the Christians would have perhaps failed in advancing the mission of Christ. As good and faithful stewards, they were also being entrepreneurial, creating and sustaining their mission work by being the church, the presence of the body of Christ in their communities. Being entrepreneurial by leveraging available resources to support ministries is good stewardship.

If these seven principles drawn from the ministry models are acted upon as appropriate for your ministry context and mission, they will bring an increased ability to engage your congregation through significant living as they experience God's call to work as the hands and feet and heart of Christ in all spheres—with God, self, others, and faith community, with the broader community and institutions, and with creation and global societies. *People are the basis of our significance.*

Notes

1. Adam Taylor, *Mobilizing Hope: Faith-Inspired Activism for A Post-Civil Rights Generation,* (Downers Grove: IVP, 2010), 189.

2. Ibid.

3. Marvin A. McMickle, *Caring Pastors, Caring People,* Living Church, ed. Dwight J. Stinnett (Valley Forge PA: Judson, 2011), 2.

4. Thomas C. Oden, cited in McMickle, *Caring Pastors, Caring People,* 2.

5. Colin Hansen, "Why Johnny Can't Read the Bible," *Christianity Today,* posted May 24, 2010, www.christianitytoday.com/ct/2010/may/25.38.html?paging=off.

CHAPTER 10

Active Spirituality and Christian Discipleship

I have presented in these pages a new paradigm for Christian discipleship lived through an active spirituality that leads to significance and experienced in living in service to others as a calling. It is a model for significant living through being present with hands-on ministry in every sphere that Acts 1:8 points us to as Christ's witnesses. I introduced a new paradigm for Christian identity. This paradigm underscored three understandings about our Christian identity: (1) discipleship is more than salvation, (2) spirituality is more than sanctification, and (3) transformation begins with our activism here and now.

I have pressed the premise throughout the book that the church is called to equip, enable, and "ordain" people to make the connections between their Christian spirituality and their souls' capacities to *touch God's creation in a personal way.* Strengthening the connection between spirituality and service for the church today is critical for disciple making in our times and times to come.

As Christian witnesses who are gifted with the power of the Holy Spirit, we are compelled to go by God's Spirit in us. Remember, the life we live through our church missions and ministries is also the life we live through our work and our communities every day, regardless of titles, degrees, positions held, group memberships, income, or financial status. To serve is our spiritual discipline. As a discipline, service makes active spirituality an essential part of Christian discipleship.

Many are seeking an oasis from all the noise and chatter of the over-networked and overstimulated environment in which we live, love, and learn. In finding ourselves overwhelmed, overcome, and overindulged, shouldn't the church extend a path of sanity where real meaning, true purpose, and deeper significance can be a life reality? This is the powerful role of the church and a fulfilling life for the believer, a life with impact.

Among the various meanings of impact, the appropriate meaning here is "the effect or impression of one thing on another."[1] We may be having an impact on someone—our families, our groups, or our communities—in one way or another, oftentimes without even having conscious intent. As we move within our various spheres, we are called by God to claim them as places where we will bring our significance and make an impact by leaving a strong impression as bearers of God's love, grace, and mercy to others, and ultimately through our having created a transformed space where God's purpose can be manifested. One of those spaces is the church itself. As churches and their members involve themselves in their surroundings in mission, service, and activism, they need to have a space where they can do as Jesus did and get away from the pressing of the crowd.

This final chapter will look at the important role of the church as an oasis.

The Importance of Balance

In response to the media saturation, the overstimulated, over networked, overinformed nature of our culture, the church has another much-needed role. While evangelism, worship, disciple making, spiritual formation, mission, and community transformation are key roles and responsibilities of the church, balance must be maintained to give people a place for the quieter, still, and contemplative needs of the Christian life. We need an oasis.

Creating Oasis

Most people living in Wisconsin and traveling south through Illinois would take Interstate 294 South. Travelers' need for respite and refueling is comforted by the appearance of a billboard indicating the exit for one of three oases travelers will come to. An oasis in Illinois is a full-service facility where travelers can gas up, eat, get highway information, use restrooms, and even loosen up in a massage chair. An oasis, whether in Illinois or elsewhere, is a welcome sight to travelers or sojourners in need. More generally, an oasis is defined as "a time or experience that is pleasant and restful; an area in a desert where there is water and plants; and a pleasant place that is surrounded by something unpleasant." Further, it is described as "a fertile green area in an arid region" and "something that provides refuge, relief, or pleasant contrast."[2]

Is this an appropriate description of a needed role for the church today? I believe it is, as the church lives amid places that are challenged. Jesus said, "Come to me, all you who are weary and burdened and I will give you *rest*" (Matthew 11:28, emphasis added), and "Let anyone who is thirsty come to me and drink" (John 7:37). These invitations create images of an oasis-like experience in the care of Jesus.

The church, being the body of Christ, is the place where individuals should experience rest or Sabbath and quenching for their thirsty souls—not only on Sunday when the church is gathered but also when the church is scattered on Monday through Saturday. What is the invitation for the body of Christ to be the pool of rest and refreshment among our spheres of significance? This question will be explored in upcoming sections that will wrap up our look at the ways our spirituality supports us as we fulfill our call to serve.

Rest—Sabbath

"Six days you shall labor, but on the seventh day you shall *rest*; even during the plowing season and harvest you must *rest*" (Exodus 34:21, emphasis added). Taking rest during the plowing and harvesting seasons was critical in the agricultural life of the Old Testament. Rest is also critical in the hustle and bustle of our times. Some of us are pressed at our jobs to accomplish more work than there are workers to handle. Workweeks, traditionally five days, too often extend themselves into the sixth day and into the evenings. We honor God by practicing sabbath, or rest, from our everyday activities. Put down your work. Give it a rest. Make space for communion with God. This is a challenge for us in our very connected, mediated, and highly stimulated culture. But this is the very reason that taking rest from our everyday pace is most beneficial to our spiritual and physical health.

What does this rest, this sabbath, look like? It may involve different practices for different people, but two common habits of holy rest stand out—worship and re-creation.

Worship. Regular participation in communal worship is a way to be in God's presence and experience God's calm and quieting of our souls. While we worship God throughout our daily lives in our personal and private devotions, worshiping in a gathered community certainly is not only a mark of Christian discipleship but is beneficial to each of us individually and to the community of faith. Attending to worship also can drive the spirit of worshipfulness in our daily rhythms.

Re-creation. Re-creation is related to what we commonly call *recreation*. To me it means to experience beginning again from the place of our sacred center, from our soul. Have you heard someone say at some point in the week, "I just wish I could begin this week again," or more so, "I just wish this week would end"? We can get to the place that we feel that bits and pieces of our authentic selves are fragmented. We need to be brought back to a greater sense of wholeness.

Because we do come to this point, *recreation* is necessary. I highly recommend that, as regularly as possible and making a disciplined commitment to do so, we each find that space that brings us back to a sacred center. For some people recreation is taking part in some form of physical activity, such as golf, skiing, or tennis. For others it is taking in a good movie with a box of popcorn, spending time reading a book or writing a poem, singing along with favorite songs, playing with younger loved ones, fishing alone or with a quiet companion, trying out a new recipe, or just enjoying a conscious quietness of their own souls. Pay attention to your own inner indicators of what brings you to be truly re-created, and do that.

Renewal

"Those who wait for the LORD shall renew their strength" (Isaiah 40:31, NRSV). To understand personal and spiritual renewal, let's use an automobile analogy. Our daily harried environment can affect us much like the harsh elements of our environment wear on our cars. Our automobiles, after months of the sun beating down on them day in and day out and being hit by pounding rain, snow, and sleet, as well as being subjected to road salt and pollutants, are left looking dull and worn. Responsible car owners know that there comes a time when they need to renew their car's finish. They wash, wax, and polish their car to bring back the shine and sparkle it once had.

Because life's everyday activities and challenges work like the environmental elements pounding our cars, we need personal renewal to restore our shine and brighten our lives. For me renewal comes when I cleanse myself from the weight of day-to-day affairs by pulling away for a while. I like to take a retreat where I can release stress, strife, struggles, and fatigue by being in the renewing presence of God's Spirit, uninterrupted. That brings back my shine! My sparkle!

I have experienced renewal as an extended time of sacred nurturing and nourishing space. As the Scripture promises, in waiting on the Lord, my strength is renewed. I am a practitioner of retreats, and my style and form of retreating varies. To retreat simply means to pull back or to come away from. Doing this does not always mean one has to leave home, take a trip, or be in any planned group experience.

I have been renewed by taking a one- or two-day period to withdraw from the intensity of my normal routine or work in exchange for a time to clear my head, free my mind, open my spirit, rest from the matters of my heart, take a nap, or walk along Lake Michigan. When I walk along the lake, God pours into me from the beauty of the water, the freshness of the air, the warmth of the sun, and the companionship of the birds, rabbits, and an occasional fish. After a time, I can feel the crustier edges that were beginning to form around my innermost parts softening and falling away into inconsequence. That doesn't mean that the weightier concerns I am carrying go away, but the heaviness of their presence is met by my increased strength. As the Scripture says, when I wait on the Lord, my strength is renewed.

Reflection

I once heard a report that people living in the twenty-first century are less reflective than persons were in previous times. To be reflective is to be thoughtful about or to give careful consideration to actions we have taken, decisions we have made, or situations we are facing. Taking the time to reflect is vital. In fact, not giving time to sincere reflection can be very dangerous for a society or an individual. When critical decisions are made with limited time given between actions, the implications of those actions may not have opportunity to surface before another decision needs to be made. As disciples of Jesus, we should well follow his pattern of "getting into the boat," "going into the garden," and asking critical questions, as he did when he asked his disciples, "Who do people say that I am?"

The apostle Paul wrote in Romans 12:1-2, teaching new believers how to live in the world as followers of Jesus, "Do not be conformed to the pattern of this world, but be transformed by the renewing of your mind. Then you will be able to test and approve what God's will is—his good, pleasing and perfect will." Giving time to be reflective is of particular importance for those who have active lifestyles. As a spiritual practice, reflection brings more than just a balance from activity; it is that central element that helps us to be clear regarding our activity and involvements, helping us to give priority and purpose to what is in alignment with God's will for us and for the people and places we serve.

Specific methods can be used in this kind of reflection that help us to check our own personal tendencies, weaknesses, egos, biases, judgments, fears, hopes, dreams, propensities, insights, questions, and answers. Being reflective is one way to inquire of our spirit if we are conformed or transformed, if our thinking is status quo or of the mind of Christ. Reflection practices may include meditating on Scripture; giving special consideration to some daily need, decision, or concern, and relating Scripture to the concern; listening for God's voice, watching for God's hand, seeing God's presence; and evaluating your response and application of the moment's revelation.

Refreshment

Peter urged his listeners in Acts 3:19-21, "Repent, then, and turn to God, so that your sins may be wiped out, that times of refreshing may come from the Lord, and that he may send the Messiah, who has been appointed for you—even Jesus. Heaven must receive him until the time comes for God to restore everything, as he promised long ago through his holy prophets."

An important part of Christian discipleship is keeping an eye on our own spiritual lives, on our "keeping right with God." We must not neglect our own propensity to sin while we are caring for our calling in the world.

Here Peter links repentance to a coming season of refreshing that comes from being in the Lord's presence. Being in the Lord's presence openly and honestly will awaken our awareness of the condition of our hearts, minds, and spirits as if a light were shined within us. Repentance, turning away from sin and seeking forgiveness, aligns us with God's season of refreshing. An oasis experience is intended for refreshment. Stopping to assess the road we are traveling and turning to go another way if necessary is good discipleship.

God's Purpose Manifested

Spirituality guides us into service that not only leads to living lives of significance but also to discovering the fulfillment of our discipleship and unique calling by God. God has something for each of us to do. Our being and our doing are singular with God's purpose in our lives and in the world. May our lives be lived in fulfillment of the prayer Jesus prayed, "Thy kingdom come; thy will be done on earth as it is in heaven." Amen.

Notes

1. *FreeDictionary.com*, s.v. "impact," accessed August 10, 2014, www.thefreedictionary.com/impact.

2. *Merriam-Webster Dictionary*, s.v. "oasis," accessed August 10, 2014, www.merriam-webster.com/dictionary/oasis.

Assessment Guide

Acts 1:8 Sphere of Significance

I invite you to assess your church's spheres of significance by using the worksheet below. Complete the response sections, considering their specific focus. The sections correlate with the Acts 1:8 Sphere of Significance diagram. A personal assessment is also made available.

Our Church's Sphere of Significance Worksheet

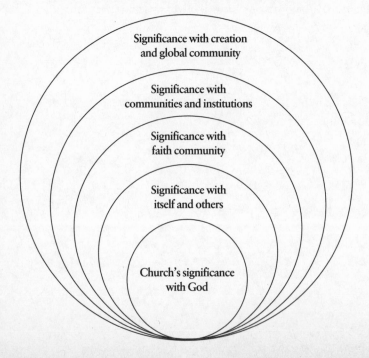

Significance with creation
and global community

Significance with
communities and institutions

Significance with
faith community

Significance with
itself and others

Church's significance
with God

1st Sphere: Church's significance with God: My church maintains our relationship with God and supports those who care for their spiritual growth through the following spiritual practices and acts of service.

Supported Spiritual Practices:

Supported Call of Service/Mission:

2nd Sphere: Significance with itself and others
Church's Inward Spiritual Practices:

Church's Outward Spiritual Practices:

3rd Sphere: Significance with faith community
Our Spiritual Practices:

Our Call of Service:

4th Sphere: Significance with communities and institutions
Our Spiritual Practices:

Our Call of Service:

5th Sphere: Significance with creation and global community
Our Spiritual Practices:

Our Call of Service:

My Personal Acts 1:8 Sphere of Significance Worksheet

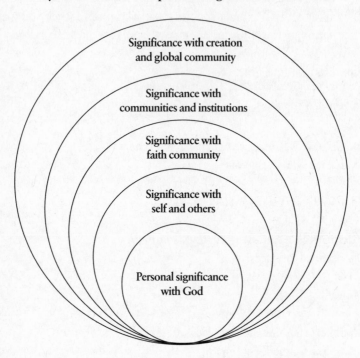

Significance with creation
and global community

Significance with
communities and institutions

Significance with
faith community

Significance with
self and others

Personal significance
with God

1st Sphere: Personal significance with God: I maintain my relationship with God and support my spiritual growth through the following spiritual practices and acts of service.

My Spiritual Practices:

My Call of Service:

2nd Sphere: Significance with self and others
My Spiritual Practices:

My Call of Service:

3rd Sphere: Significance with faith community
My Spiritual Practices:

My Call of Service:

4th Sphere: Significance with communities and institutions
My Spiritual Practices:

My Call of Service:

5th Sphere: Significance with creation and global community
My Spiritual Practices:

My Call of Service: